The
Chow Chow

An Owner's Guide To

A HAPPY HEALTHY PET

Howell Book House

Howell Book House
A Simon & Schuster Macmillan Company
1633 Broadway
New York, NY 10019

Library of Congress Cataloging-in-Publication Data
Braun, Paulette
The Chow Chow: An Owner's Guide to a Happy Healthy Pet
p. cm.
Includes bibliographical references.
ISBN 0-87605-390-8
1. Chow chows (Dogs) I. Title.
SF429.C5B735 1996   95-52288
636.7'2—dc20   CIP

Manufactured in the United States of America
10 9 8 7 6 5 4 3 2

Series Director: Dominique De Vito
Series Assistant Director: Ariel Cannon
Book Design: Michele Laseau
Cover Design: Iris Jeromnimon
Illustration: Jeff Yesh
Photography:
    Cover: Paulette Braun/Pets by Paulette
    Courtesy of the American Kennel Club: 16, 20
    Mary Bloom: 96, 136, 145
    Paulette Braun/Pets by Paulette: 2–3, 5, 7, 11, 15, 22, 27, 29, 30, 32, 33, 34, 38–39, 40, 42, 43, 45, 46, 47, 48, 53, 54, 59, 61, 62, 65, 66, 67, 69, 73, 81, 91, 94
    Buckinghamhill American Cocker Spaniels: 148
    Sian Cox: 134
    Dr. Ian Dunbar: 98, 101, 103, 111, 116–117, 122, 123, 127
    Dan Lyons: 96
    Scott McKiernan: 9, 25, 26
    Cathy Merrithew: 129
    Liz Palika: 133
    Janice Raines: 132
    Judith Strom: 13, 96, 107, 110, 128, 130, 135, 137, 139, 140, 144, 149, 150
    Kerrin Winter & Dale Churchill: 96–97
Production Team: Trudy Brown, Jama Carter, Kathleen Caulfield, Trudy Coler, Amy De Angelis, Pete Fornatale, Matt Hannafin, Kathy Iwasaki, Vic Peterson, Terri Sheehan, Marvin Van Tiem, and Kathleen Varanese

Contents

Welcome
to the
World
of the

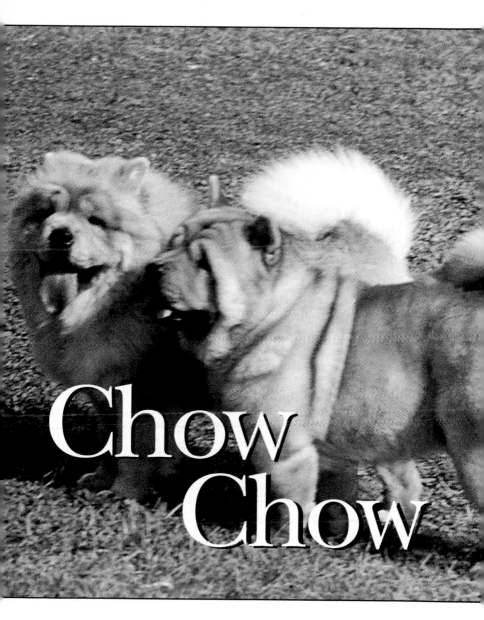

part one

Chow Chow

External Features of the Chow Chow

chapter 1

What
Is a
Chow Chow?

The Chow Chow is a dignified, discriminating dog with a serious, scowling expression and a distinctive black or bluish-black tongue and mouth. His lavish coat is accentuated by a lionlike ruff framing a massive yet elegantly carried head. Medium-sized, although his coat makes him appear larger, the Chow Chow has heavy bones and strong, solid muscle. He moves with a unique stilted gait and carries his tail on top of his back, close to the spine. The breed comes in two coat types—the profusely coated **rough,** and the rarer **smooth**.

An ancient breed of Chinese origin, the Chow Chow was once used to hunt tigers and bears. Today, the breed is in the AKC Group called

Non-Sporting, a sort of catch-all group for dogs whose original purpose has been phased out by the advance of civilization, as well as breeds that were always loved solely as companions.

The Breed Standard

Every breed has a "standard" that thoroughly explains its appearance. Written by the national club that represents the breed, the standard is like a blueprint in words, describing in detail how the ideal specimen of that breed should look. Reputable breeders think of the standard as an explanation of perfection, and strive to produce animals that come as close to it as possible.

Studying the breed standard is the best way to learn the distinguishing characteristics of a breed. The following is an explanation of the Standard of the Chow Chow as approved by the American Kennel Club in 1986. Actual quotes from the standard are printed in italics, and explanations and comments are in regular type. To help you understand the Chow Chow, this chapter accentuates features that are unique to the breed. For a copy of the complete AKC Standard for the Chow Chow, write to the American Kennel Club, 5580 Centerview Dr., Raleigh, NC 27690-0643.

> ### WHAT IS A BREED STANDARD?
>
> A breed standard—a detailed description of an individual breed—is meant to portray the *ideal* specimen of that breed. This includes ideal structure, temperament, gait, type—all aspects of the dog. Because the standard describes an ideal specimen, it isn't based on any particular dog. It is a concept against which judges compare actual dogs and breeders strive to produce dogs. At a dog show, the dog that wins is the one that comes closest, in the judge's opinion, to the standard for its breed. Breed standards are written by the breed parent clubs, the national organizations formed to oversee the well-being of the breed. They are voted on and approved by the members of the parent clubs.

Starting at the Top

Head—*Proudly carried, large in proportion to the size of the dog but never so exaggerated as to make the dog seem top-heavy or to result in a low carriage.*

The Chow Chow should be a balanced dog. While his head immediately attracts attention with its large size and exotic expression, it should not be so huge as to overpower the rest of the dog. Also, the Chow properly carries his head in a rather haughty fashion, so the head should never be so massive as to weigh the dog down and prevent him from appearing elegant. On the other hand, the head should never seem small in comparison to the dog's large bones, muscular body and lavish coat.

Expression—*Essentially scowling, dignified, lordly, discerning, sober and snobbish, one of independence.*

Although the Chow Chow really is an independent dog, his individualistic look is the result of a combination of physical features, not his attitude. The dog appears to be scowling due to a padded button of skin just above the inner corner of each eye, as well as skin on the forehead just loose enough to form the wrinkle that produces the frowning aspect. His brow marking also contributes to the expression as does a noticeable furrow that begins at the base of the muzzle and runs up the forehead. The natural frown turns into an inscrutable oriental scowl thanks to the dog's widely spaced dark eyes, which are almond shaped and obliquely set.

The Chow Chow's head is large and exotic, with furrows of skin contributing to his unique expression.

The Chow Chow's eye rims should be black, with the pupils of the eyes clearly visible, not hidden by loosely hanging skin. The lids should not turn in or out and shouldn't droop. This is extremely important, because entropion (lids that turn in, causing hair to irritate the cornea) can lead to excessive tearing, or even loss of sight due to scarring. Ectropion (loose bottom lids that turn outward and droop) also lead to trouble. Hanging lower lids collect airborne irritants, resulting in red, inflamed eyes.

Ears—*Small, moderately thick, triangular in shape, with a slight rounding at the tip, carried stiffly erect but with a slight*

*forward tilt. Placed wide apart with the inner corner on
top of the skull. An ear which flops as the dog moves is very
undesirable.*

In the showring, a Chow with a drop ear or with both
ears drooping will be disqualified from competition. A
drop ear is one that bends at any point from its base to
its tip, or one that hangs or droops in any direction.
Proper carriage for the Chow Chow ear is fully and
stiffly erect.

If your Chow Chow puppy is still very young and has
ears that hang like a Labrador Retriever's, you may be
able to help them stand erect. Sometimes a young
puppy's ears don't stand because they are too heavy
with hair, and it's worth a try to clip the hair off the
puppy's ears. Sure your puppy will look raggedy for
awhile, but hair grows back, and by the time it does the
ear cartilage will probably be strong enough to hold it
proudly erect. Don't panic if your Chow puppy's ears
go limp during teething time. They will eventually
point skyward again on their own.

The top of a Chow's head should be broad and flat.
The **muzzle** should be short in comparison to the
length of the top of the skull, but not exceedingly
short. It should also be broad, and appear quite square
when viewed from the front. This square aspect comes
from good bone structure, full, rather thick lips and
proper padding around the muzzle. When the Chow's
mouth is closed, his upper lips should cover his lower
lips, but the lips should not be so large or loose that
they hang slack.

The Chow has a large, broad **nose** and well-opened
nostrils. Any color nose other than solid black is considered faulty. The exceptions are blue Chows; they
may have slate-gray or solid-blue noses.

The **teeth** should appear strong and even and meet in
a scissors bite (upper front teeth meeting tightly outside the lower front teeth).

Mouth and Tongue—*Edges of the lips black, tissues of the
mouth mostly black, gums preferably black. A solid black*

mouth is ideal. The top surface and edges of the tongue a solid blue-black, the darker the better.

One of the hallmarks of the Chow Chow is that famous tongue and mouth. Therefore, if the edges of the tongue are pink or red, or even spotted with pink or red, the dog will be disqualified from dog show competition. But don't fret if your puppy still has some pink showing on her tongue or mouth. Most Chow puppies are born with a pink tongue and a nose that is lighter than black. Nose and mouth pigmentation darkens gradually, and its speed varies a great deal between puppies. One puppy may have dark pigment by a month old, while another puppy's pigment may not fill in completely until the dog is eight or ten months of age.

FEET, LEGS AND MOVEMENT

Forequarters—*Shoulders strong, well muscled, the tips of the shoulder blades moderately close together; the spine of the shoulder forms an angle approximately 55 degrees with the horizontal and forms an angle with the upper arm of approximately 110 degrees, resulting in less reach of the forelegs. Length of upper arm never less than length of shoulder blade. Elbow joints set well back alongside the chest wall, elbows turning neither in nor out.*

The Chow Chow's blue-black tongue is a distinct characteristic of the breed.

The Chow Chow's **shoulders** should appear powerful, and the angle formed at the point where the shoulder bone meets the upper arm bone is a straighter angle than that found in almost all other breeds.

Ideal **elbows** are right alongside the wall of the chest, and they should neither point in toward the floor of the chest nor protrude outward.

Good **front legs** appear sturdy and strong-boned but are not so thick that they are out of proportion with the rest of the dog. They should be absolutely straight from the elbow to the foot, and spaced wide enough to be in perfect balance with the dog's broad chest. When seen from the front, the forelegs should be perfectly parallel to each other. Legs that appear closer at the top with the feet spread wide (like a tripod) are incorrect, and so are feet that turn in or out. Pasterns should be short and straight. Dewclaws may be removed.

The configuration of the dog's **feet** is also very important. The Chow Chow's feet should not be large for her size and ideally are compact, round and well-arched like a cat's paw. Long, thin toes and splayed feet (flat, with space between the toes) are both undesirable. The Chow should stand well up on her feet, and her toe pads should be thick to cushion her movement. You can help keep your dog's feet in good shape by regularly clipping her toenails. Chapter 6 tells you how.

Good Chow Chow **hindquarters** are powerful and broad, with well-muscled hips and thighs. The rear legs should have heavy bone. In fact, the rear leg bones should be just as heavy as the front leg bones for a well-balanced aspect. When seen from the rear, the legs should appear straight and perfectly parallel, and widely spaced enough to be in proportion with the dog's broad pelvis. Cow-hocked rear legs (hocks pointing toward each other), bowed legs (hocks pointing out to each side), and rear legs placed too close

THE AMERICAN KENNEL CLUB

Familiarly referred to as "the AKC," the American Kennel Club is a nonprofit organization devoted to the advancement of purebred dogs. The AKC maintains a registry of recognized breeds and adopts and enforces rules for dog events including shows, obedience trials, field trials, hunting tests, lure coursing, herding, earthdog trials, agility and the Canine Good Citizen program. It is a club of clubs, established in 1884 and composed, today, of over 500 autonomous dog clubs throughout the United States. Each club is represented by a delegate; the delegates make up the legislative body of the AKC, voting on rules and electing directors. The American Kennel Club maintains the Stud Book, the record of every dog ever registered with the AKC, and publishes a variety of materials on purebred dogs, including a monthly magazine, books and numerous educational pamphlets. For more information, contact the AKC at the address listed in Chapter 13, "Resources," and look for the names of their publications in Chapter 12, "Recommended Reading."

together (usually caused by a pelvis that is too narrow) are all considered faulty.

Stifle Joint—*It shows little angulation, is well knit and stable, and points straight forward; and the bones of the joint should be clean and sharp.* **Hock Joint** *well let down and appears almost straight. The hock joint must be strong, well knit and firm, never bowing or breaking forward or to either side. The hock joint and metatarsals lie in a straight line below the hip joint.* **Serious Faults**—*Unsound stifle or hock joints. Metatarsals short and perpendicular to the ground. The dewclaws may be removed. Feet same as front.*

Did you ever hear the phrase, "crooked as a dog's hind leg?" Well, that doesn't apply to the Chow Chow.

A dog's hind leg has an upper and lower thigh, separated by the stifle joint (knee to us), which is located on the frontal part of the dog's hind leg. The rear drive that pushes most dogs forward comes from flexing and straight-ening the stifle. A stifle with little angulation (as described in the Chow standard) shortens a dog's stride, making for a choppy gait. That's why the standards for almost all other breeds demand a well-angulated or moderately angulated stifle. The Chow's straight hock (joint between the stifle and the foot) is also unique, as this joint is also well-angulated on almost all other breeds. The bones connecting the hock to the feet are the metatarsals, and they must also be straight.

The Chow Chow is a square-shaped dog with a straight topline and powerful rump.

Because the Chow's rear legs are shaped differently than other dogs' rear legs, the Chow Chow's **gait** is distinctive. No one knows for certain why the breed evolved with its characteristic stilted movement, but some historians surmise that this attribute may have helped the earliest Chow Chows maneuver through deep snow. The standard describes the movement resulting from the straight stifles and hocks as follows:

Gait—*Proper movement is the crucial test of proper conformation and soundness. It must be sound, straight-moving, agile, brief, quick and powerful, never lumbering. The rear gait short and stilted because of the straighter rear assembly. It is from the side that the unique stilted action is most easily assessed. The rear leg moves up and forward from the hip in a straight, stilted pendulumlike line with a slight bounce in the rump; the legs extend neither far forward nor far backward. The hind foot has a strong thrust which transfers power to the body in an almost straight line due to the minimal rear leg angulation. To transmit this power efficiently to the front assembly, the coupling must be short and there should be no roll through the mid-section. Viewed from the rear, the line of bone from hip joint to pad remains straight as the dog moves. As the speed increases, the hind legs incline slightly inward. The stifle joints must point in the line of travel, not outward (resulting in a bowlegged appearance) nor hitching in under the dog. Viewed from the front, the line of bone from shoulder joint to pad remains straight as the dog moves. As the speed increases, the forelegs do not move in exact parallel planes, rather, incline slightly inward. The front legs must not swing out in semicircles nor mince nor show any evidence of hackney action. The front and rear assemblies must be in dynamic equilibrium. Somewhat lacking in speed, the Chow has excellent endurance because the sound, straight rear leg provides direct, usable power efficiently.*

When you watch a Chow come toward you, his front legs should remain in a straight line from the shoulder to the toes when the dog is trotting slowly. At speed, the legs still remain straight but tend to converge, inclining slightly toward the middle of the dog. If the front legs are lifted noticeably high (hackney action), swing out to the side, or toe in or out, the Chow's movement is faulty.

The back legs, when seen from the rear, remain straight from the hip to the feet when the dog is moving. As the dog trots faster, the rear legs will converge (incline inward) just as the front legs do.

Rear leg faults include hocks that turn in (sometimes so much that the rear legs interfere with each other), and hocks that turn outward or bow, making the feet point inward.

When a Chow Chow moves well, there is no wasted motion. His feet stay close to the ground, propelling the dog with short, brisk steps and his midsection does not roll.

The Body Beautiful

The Chow Chow is a medium-sized dog with heavy bone and strong muscular development. Fine-boned, snipy (long and pointy muzzled) specimens, and massive, clumsy specimens are equally faulty. Females may have less body substance and smaller heads than do males. The average height for mature Chows is 17 to 20 inches at the withers.

Neck, Topline, Body—*Neck strong, full, well muscled, nicely arched and of sufficient length to carry the head proudly above the topline when standing at attention. Topline straight, strong and level from the withers to the root of the tail.*

The top of a dog's back, from the withers (top of the shoulders) to the root of the tail (where the tail meets the body), is called the **topline**. While many breeds are supposed to have a sloping topline (one that is higher at the withers than at the croup or rump), this is not the case with the Chow Chow. This breed's standard calls for a topline that is both straight and sturdy.

Because of the way he's built, the Chow has a unique gait that propels him forward in a strong, straight style.

The ideal Chow's body is broad, deep, well-muscled, short and compact. Likewise, the impressive chest should also be wide, deep and muscular. Such a chest, along with close, well-sprung ribs, allows ample room and plenty of protection for housing the heart and lungs. Both a narrow chest and the labored or

13

abdominal breathing that might result from insufficient chest space are considered serious faults.

In profile, the Chow Chow should present a square appearance. This is achieved when the distance from the withers to the ground is equal to the distance from the forechest (point of the chest) to the point of the buttock (the back of the upper rear leg). According to the Chow standard, any profile other than square is a serious fault. Other recommended proportions essential to the special look of a Chow include: The distance from the tip of the elbow to the ground should equal half the dog's height (first measure from the elbow to the ground, then measure from the withers to the ground and divide by two); the floor (bottom) of the chest (sometimes referred to as the brisket) should be level with the point of the elbow; the width of the dog viewed from the front should be the same as the width of the dog viewed from the rear, and both should be broad.

The Chow's rump and thigh muscles should be powerful. The tail is ideally set high on the back and should always be carried on top of the back close to the spine.

The Crowning Glory: The Coat

The Chow Chow's luxurious coat completes the exquisite picture.

Coat—*There are two types of coat, rough and smooth. Both are double coated.*

Rough—*In the rough coat, the outer coat is abundant, dense, straight and offstanding, rather coarse in texture; the undercoat, soft, thick and wooly. Puppy coat soft, thick and wooly overall. The coat forms a profuse ruff around the head and neck, framing the head. The coat and ruff generally longer in dogs than in bitches. Tail well-feathered. The coat length varies markedly on different Chows, and thickness, texture and condition should be given greater emphasis than length. Obvious trimming or shaping is undesirable. Trimming of the whiskers, feet and metatarsals optional.*

Smooth—*The smooth coated Chow is judged by the same standard as the rough coated Chow except that references to the quantity and distribution of the outer coat are not applicable to the smooth coated Chow, which has a hard, dense, smooth outer coat with a definite undercoat. There should be no obvious ruff or feathering on the legs or tail.*

Chow Chows come in five **colors**, and two of those colors come in an array of attractive hues. Acceptable colors are red (which may vary from light golden to deep mahogany), cinnamon (light fawn to deep cinnamon), cream, blue and black. In addition, a color may be clear, solid, or solid with lighter shadings in the ruff, tail and feathering.

All-Important Temperament

In the final analysis, correct temperament is the most important attribute of all. Physical beauty alone never compensates for lack of character or the correct disposition for the breed.

Temperament—*Keen intelligence, an independent spirit and innate dignity give the Chow an aura of aloofness. It is a Chow's nature to be reserved and discerning with strangers. Displays of aggression or timidity are unacceptable. Because of its deep set eyes, the Chow has limited peripheral vision and is best approached within the scope of that vision.*

The rough Chow has an abundant outer coat, whereas the smooth has a hard, dense outer coat. The differences are obvious in this photo of the two together.

While good breeding leads to good temperament, all puppies must be socialized so that the potential for proper temperament that was bred into them can emerge. Chapter 4 explains the important process of socialization.

15

chapter 2

The
Chow Chow's
Ancestry

Since ancient Chinese emperors routinely destroyed every piece of art and literature from the preceding dynasty, the early history of the Chow Chow is as inscrutable as its expression. Legends of the 11th-century B.C. invasion of China by the Tartar hordes tell of huge lionlike dogs with black tongues who attacked the Chinese warriors, bringing them down to their knees for the barbarians to kill. Later, when relations between the Chow Dynasty and the invaders became friendly, the barbarians offered some of these war dogs as tribute.

One of the Oldest of Breeds

Although there are few descriptions of these ancient dogs, there is agreement among historians that the dogs were large, strong, and had profuse coats that were most often red. Those who agree with the theory of the Chow Chow's arrival in the courts of the Chinese emperors also believe that those early dogs were off-shoots of some of the most primitive species and therefore a basic breed, one of the oldest breeds on earth.

According to this explanation, the Chow Chow is the original ancestor of all Spitz-type dogs (nordic dogs characterized by prick ears, tails curled over their backs, double coats and wedge-shaped muzzles). Originating in the Arctic Circle as a breed somewhere between a dog and a bear, the woolly, red animal eventually migrated to eastern Asia. There the dogs lived and multiplied in ancient Mongolia until partially domesticated by the nomadic, warlike tribes who eventually attacked China.

Historians who consider this theory plausible point out that no other animal on earth, except a few rare Asiatic bears and, to a lesser degree, the polar bear, has the peculiar bluish-black tongue, and that these unique animals all had origins in the same part of the world. This doctrine also mentions meager records of Chinese antiquity (those few that survived each new emperor's decree of destruction), which considered the large, hairy, black-tongued dog an oddity and a for-eigner, and labeled him the "man kow," which roughly translates to "the barbarian's dog."

A piece of pot-tery from the Han Dynasty in 206 B.C. has an unmis-takable Chow shape.

There are additional theories. Some historians hypoth-esize that the Chow Chow evolved from crosses of the

Samoyed with the ancient Mastiff of Tibet. Still others conclude that today's Chow Chow is the original Mastiff of Tibet, and thus an ancestor of the Samoyed, Keeshond, Norwegian Elkhound and Pomeranian.

Finding the Facts

We know for certain that the Chow Chow breed is over 2,000 years old. Bas-relief sculpture and pottery dating to the Han Dynasty (207 B.C. to A.D. 220) give absolute proof that the Chow Chow was a versatile Chinese hunting dog at least that long ago. Formidable on big game such as bear and tiger, the breed was also prized for its ability to scent, point and retrieve Mongolian pheasant and quail. By A.D. 700, an early T'ang emperor of the Yunan Province kept a kennel of 5,000 Chowlike hunting dogs and a staff of 10,000 huntsmen—one of the most colossal kennel establishments ever recorded.

Guard and Shepherd Artwork from this period most often depicted the Chow as part of the Imperial Hunt, but the dog was also esteemed as a fierce guard and alert shepherd. His work included protecting caravans and serving as sentry on sampans and junks. In addition, "The Book of Marco Polo" relates that the dogs were used to pull sledges in the manner of other Nordic breeds.

Food and Fetish Dog flesh was a favorite dish in China, so besides breeding Chows for their working qualities, the Chinese also raised the dogs for meat and made clothing from the fur of the longhaired variety. Puppies were fattened on rice, other grains and vegetables, then slaughtered when young.

But while these dogs were the main course in Canton and throughout most of China, the breed had religious significance in a few locales, and in some cases, still does. Since the 13th century A.D. a special strain of Chows has been carefully bred in some remote and mountainous Chinese monasteries with every breeding recorded for several hundred years. The dogs are prized for the dual purpose of guarding and hunting, and in some temples, the blue-colored Chow is considered holy and receives special care from the monks. An outsider had the rare privilege of witnessing the results of the monks' work when one Dr. Abshegen was permitted to visit a Lamist monastery during the period when the Japanese occupied Northern China. Later, he recorded his visit in an essay entitled, "The Blue Chows of Mongolia." According to his work, the monastery bred its own strain of "heavenly blue" dogs. Dr. Abshegen also said he heeded the monks' warning about the protectiveness of the pack by carrying a club when he visited.

Emigration to England

Because of China's closed-door policy, the Chow Chow did not leave China for centuries. Finally, during the latter part of the 18th century, a few Chows were smuggled to England by sailors. The British took an immediate interest in the mysterious Chow Chow when he arrived on their shores. With his lionlike ruff, blue-black tongue and scowling expression, the breed was considered an exotic oddity. Also, the dogs were used to a vegetarian diet and often refused to eat the meat commonly fed dogs in England. Some of the earliest Chows to reach England were housed in the London Zoological Garden and labeled "the wild dogs of China."

WHERE DID DOGS COME FROM?

It can be argued that dogs were right there at man's side from the beginning of time. As soon as human beings began to document their existence, the dog was among their drawings and inscriptions. Dogs were not just friends, they served a purpose: There were dogs to hunt birds, pull sleds, herd sheep, burrow after rats—even sit in laps! What your dog was originally bred to do influences the way it behaves. The American Kennel Club recognizes over 140 breeds, and there are hundreds more distinct breeds around the world. To make sense of the breeds, they are grouped according to their size or function. The AKC has seven groups:

1) Sporting, 2) Working,
3) Herding, 4) Hounds,
5) Terriers, 6) Toys,
7) Nonsporting

Can you name a breed from each group? Here's some help: (1) Golden Retriever; (2) Doberman Pinscher; (3) Collie; (4) Beagle; (5) Scottish Terrier; (6) Maltese; and (7) Dalmatian. All modern domestic dogs (Canis familiaris) are related, however different they look, and are all descended from Canis lupus, the gray wolf.

THE QUEEN'S FAVORITE

In 1865, the Chow Chow's luck changed in England. That was the year Queen Victoria received a Chow puppy as a gift. Instead of having it kenneled and looking upon it as a bizarre curiosity, the Queen was smitten by the precious ball of orange fluff and made the puppy her constant companion. According to some sagas, the Queen's ladies-in-waiting were concerned about her strong attachment to her beloved pet and devised a plan that they thought would not only please her but provide her with something more healthy to cuddle than a real live dog. They paid a dressmaker to create a stuffed dog that looked just like the Queen's Chow puppy and presented it to the Queen. Because it weighed less and was cleaner (in their minds) than a real dog, they thought it would be better for her to pet and hug. Rumor has it the Queen was pleased with the gift but preferred to continue petting the dog who returned her affection. In fact, she eventually acquired a second live pet Chow.

Ch. Ledgeland's Kan Kan, whelped in 1942.

The English Chow Chow Club was organized in 1895 and established the first standard for the breed. For the next several years the English breeders met the demand for Chows in other countries, such as France, Belgium and the United States.

How the Chow Chow Got Its Name

One theory of how the Chow Chow got his name is that "chow" or "chou" is Chinese slang for "edible." However, since the Chinese themselves referred to these dogs by a variety of names, such as Hei She-t'ou (black-tongued), Hsiung Kou (bear dog), Lang Kou (wolf dog) and Kwantung Kou (Cantonese dog), it's doubtful that the breed's modern name came from the Chinese at all.

Most historians believe the breed was inadvertently named by the cargo masters of the East India Company's clipper ships. This company did much trade with China during the late 18th century—a period when the English and French were infatuated by things Chinese and anxious to purchase oriental jewelry, rugs, paintings, porcelain dolls and ivory figurines. The holds of the clipper ships that brought these goods, as well as miscellaneous items such as mixed pickles, to the British Isles were called "chow chow" holds. Rather than listing each individual item on the bill of lading, the cargo masters often listed everything that was going into a "chow chow" hold as simply "chow chow." Since the Chinese dogs imported to England rode in those holds, they came to be called Chow Chow—and so did the mixed pickles.

Arrival in America

During the latter 19th century, a few Chow Chows were imported to the United States from England. The initial arrivals were regarded as novelties, but soon a few proud owners began exhibiting them at dog shows.

The first Chow to be shown in America was named Takya. Owned by Miss A. C. Derby, he placed third in the Miscellaneous Class at the 1890 Westminster Kennel Club show in New York City. An English import named Chinese Chum was the first American Champion. He won his championship title in 1905 and sired the second American Champion, Night of Asia.

Both were owned by Mrs. Charles E. Proctor's famed Blue Dragon Kennels.

Though still a rare sight at dog shows, by the turn of the century, Chow Chows were becoming popular in the United States. In 1905 a pair of Chows, Ch. Red Idol and Illswango, were named Best Brace in Show at a dog show in Philadelphia. They were owned by Dr. and Mrs. Henry Jarrett, who were instrumental in organizing Chow enthusiasts to form a national club for the breed. The American Kennel Club officially recognized the breed in 1903, and Yen How was the first AKC registered Chow. The Chow Chow Club of America was established and became an AKC member club in 1906.

The Chinese referred to Chows by a variety of names, including "Hsiung Kou," or Bear Dog. Shown are a cream rough and two shaded red smooth dogs.

Exhibiting at dog shows eventually became a popular pastime for Chow Chow owners and breeders, and there was friendly rivalry between fanciers of imported dogs and owners of dogs bred in America. World War I slowed down the breeding and exhibiting of all breeds, but following the war, Chow owners once again debated the virtues of imports and homebreds and tried to prove their point in the showring.

Most of the early owners and breeders of Chow Chows in the United States were quite wealthy. One of the dogs imported to the United States from England cost the phenomenal price of 1,800 pounds sterling, or the equivalent of $10,000. Fortunately, Ch. Choonam

Brilliantine of Manchoover did his new owner, Mrs. Earl Hoover, proud. A champion in England and America, he sired fourteen champions and is considered an important foundation sire of the breed.

Another eminent foundation sire in America was Ch. Win Sum Min T'sing. He was bred by Mr. Franklin Hutton, who was the father of Barbara Hutton, heiress of the Woolworth fortune.

How Popularity Harms

President Calvin Coolidge had two pet Chow Chows, Tiny Tim and Blackberry, and their presence in the White House from 1923 to 1929 increased the public's awareness of this unique breed. The Chow Chow's popularity soared during the 1920s and ascended even higher during the '30s. Since sudden popularity always harms a breed, this was a difficult period for loyal lovers of the Chow. Those who had spent years practicing the highest caliber of selective breeding watched in horror as fly-by-night Chow owners exploited their beloved breed. Using inferior sires and dams as breeding stock, these profiteers sold poor-quality, unsocialized puppies to an unsuspecting public for a prodigious profit.

By the late '30s, poor breeding practices resulted in a bad reputation for the Chow Chow. "Nasty," people said. "Bad-tempered and sickly." Soon the public found a new fad breed, and the unscrupulous breeders jumped on that bandwagon, leaving the Chow Chows' faithful followers the task of restoring their breed's quality and reputation. It was a labor of love, and they did it well. For the next several decades, dedicated Chow breeders preserved and perfected the distinctive characteristics of their dogs, socialized their puppies and helped new owners learn proper Chow Chow care.

American Success Stories

Healthy and temperamentally sound again, the Chow thrived in America for almost the next forty years: from the early 1940s to the late '70s. Meanwhile, back

**FAMOUS
OWNERS OF
CHOW CHOWS**

Queen
Victoria

President
Calvin
Coolidge

Elvis Presley

Sigmund
Freud

Howard Baker

Sally Struthers

Heather
Locklear

in the showring, the Chow Chows born in America were starting to edge the imported stock out of the ribbons, according to an article by Mrs. William S. Baer that appeared in the Chow Chow Club's 1932 Show Catalogue and Year Book. The work include statistics, so it could not be dismissed as just one writer's opinion.

A book about a Chow, *The Memoirs of Chi-Chi*, was published during the thirties. It was written by Chi-Chi's owner, Mrs. Berry Wall, although the storyteller in the book was Chi-Chi. The work was particularly interesting because the Walls were international travelers, rather like jet-setters before jets, and had had a myriad of exciting experiences. Chi-Chi was so well known among the rich and famous that when he died, at the age of sixteen, his obituary appeared in French newspapers.

Even Elvis had a Chow, a red male named Gitlow. When the dog was diagnosed with a critical kidney ailment that couldn't be treated in Memphis, Elvis had his private pilot fly Gitlow to a clinic in Boston. Unfortunately the dog died and Elvis was devastated.

Other celebrities who owned (or currently own) Chow Chows include Dr. Sigmund Freud; Ohio Senator Wayne Hayes; Governor of Pennsylvania Milton Shapp; Howard Baker, President Reagan's Chief of Staff; Ron Glass of the television show "Barney Miller"; Sally Struthers of "All in the Family" fame; and Heather Locklear of "Dynasty" and "Melrose Place."

During the early seventies, Chow Chows ranked 44th in popularity among AKC breeds, placing them on the high side of the middle on a popularity chart. It was a logical position for a fine but unique breed—one that most definitely isn't right for everyone. Potential buyers who had done their research could easily find an excellent kennel where they could purchase a healthy, socialized puppy with the proper disposition. In most cases, the breeder was delighted to double as mentor, helping the new owner learn proper puppy care. Well-bred and properly raised, Chow Chows served well as charming companions, show dogs and guardians.

A Recurring Nightmare

Due to an incredible surge in popularity, the eighties became buyer-beware time again: The nightmare of fad status revisited the breed. In 1979, Chows ended the decade as the twenty-sixth most numerous breed, and by 1981 they attained top-twenty popularity, with a ranking of seventeen. By then, quick-buck breeders, using defective dogs to turn out inferior puppies, outnumbered those who traditionally bred with care and pride.

If there was any question that the Chow was headed for another disaster, it was answered in 1982, when the breed jumped four positions, to the thirteenth-most-popular AKC breed. Public demand for the blue-tongued teddy was still relentless, and by 1986 the Chow Chow, a long-haired (usually) dog that needs regular coat care and must be well socialized, was the sixth most popular dog in America. That year alone, 43,026 Chow Chows were registered. Soon veterinarians complained that the Chow was the worst-tempered to treat of all breeds, and owners complained about disagreeable dispositions and a myriad of health problems. Of course, lovely, healthy Chow Chows still existed, because excellent breeders still existed, but for several years they were vastly outnumbered by the profiteers.

Starting in the 1930s, American-bred show dogs started winning over their imported ancestors. Today the Chow is still a popular show dog.

By the late eighties, many disillusioned first-time Chow owners said, "Never again!" and the breed's popularity began to decline. From seventh in 1990, it dropped to ninth in 1991.

Serendipitous Statistics

"The Chow is now on the downside of the fad roller coaster that has quickly taken numerous other breeds to the top of the registration rankings, only to see them fall as fast as they rose," American Kennel Club Vice President, John Mandeville, wrote in the April 1992 issue of the *AKC Gazette*.

Happily for the breed, his prediction was correct. From the tenth spot in 1992, it dropped to fifteenth in 1993 and seventeenth in 1994. Commenting on the Chow Chow's decrease, Mandeville wrote for the *Gazette* of April 1995: "The American public almost always has a fad breed. Invariably, such breeds have unique and appealing qualities. They also have attributes that do not really make them candidates for mass popularity. The result is a sharp increase in popularity and an equally sharp decline."

The Chow Chow's popularity surged in the 1980s. It is currently receding, and the Chow's future seems safe in the hands of breeders who truly love it.

When numbers decrease, quality increases. Those who carefully bred Chows before they became fashionable, and their disciples, are still with us. They never bought a ticket for the roller-coaster ride and always bred for quality, not quantity. And when the public developed a poor perception of their breed, they continued loving their dogs and showing their dogs, proving through example that the real Chow Chow—the breed that endured tiger hunts, voyages in the holds of clipper ships, zoos, and overpopulation— was still beautiful, still stable, still functional, and still not for everyone.

chapter 3

The **World**

According to the
Chow Chow

To understand how the Chow Chow relates to his world, we have to look at what the Chow Chow was brought into the world to do.

We know he is the ancestor of all spitz-type dogs, a hardy creature who originated in the Arctic Circle, where he looked as much like a bear as a dog. His first human families were the nomadic, warring Mongolians of Eastern Asia. Foreigners called this ancient Chow Chow "the barbarian's dog."

In China, he was selectively bred as a hunter, guard dog and shepherd. His appearance was always part of his appeal, and when he eventually made it to England, his exotic looks made him an instant hit. On Western shores, at least, the Chow Chow has been bred as a companion dog for over two centuries.

But his teddy-bear appeal still remains only part of the package that is the Chow Chow.

Dignified, Reserved and Devoted

Underneath that gorgeous coat is a formidable dog— the hunter and shepherd of generations. The Chow Chow puppy is a playful, active, outgoing ball of fluff, but as he grows older, he becomes more aloof. He becomes the "independent," "dignified" dog that's described in the breed standard: "reserved and discerning with strangers."

If it's a Frisbee-catching, group-loving, lie-at-your-feet-at-night best friend you want, you'll have to find another breed. If it's a devoutly loyal, free-thinking, undemanding, neat, proud and noble beauty you're after, the Chow Chow's the dog for you. In fact, despite his seeming aloofness, the Chow Chow bonds so quickly and so thoroughly with his family that it's very difficult for him to change homes. Adopted Chow Chows sometimes take months to readjust, and owners have reported they seem to look for former owners even years later.

Excellent House Dogs

Shoo Li will let you know quite early on that he is not an outdoor dog. His idea of a good time is not to frolic in the yard or keep squirrels off the property. What he loves is to be around you, but not on top of you. He is happiest snoozing in his "spot" in the house or apartment while you buzz around doing whatever it is you need to do. He will know where you are, and he doesn't need to follow you around slavishly.

If your routine takes you to the corner for the newspaper in the morning, he'll gladly accompany you and relieve himself on the way—preferably in the farthest corner from the house (he is a very clean dog). If you need to go to the bank, then run some quick errands, there's nothing he would like more than to accompany you. He'll assume his post in the car and carefully and quietly watch everything that happens. Remember, Chows overheat *very quickly*. If you live in a warm climate, *do not leave your Chow unattended in a closed car.* Even if you leave the windows open slightly, try not to be gone from the car for more than a few minutes.

If it's a devoted, undemanding, beautiful and hairy dog you want, the Chow's for you.

Back at home, he'll appreciate a short stroll in his yard (on leash, please, or inside a fenced area), but short is the key word. Let him inside with you, and he'll resume his spot and again be out of your way. If a stranger comes to the door, he'll bark; he's very protective of his family. But if it's someone you let inside, don't think he'll be excited about it. Instead, he'll go back and lie down. Considering what a good-sized, hairy dog he is, you often won't know Shoo Li is there.

Rain Haters

If you think Shoo Li doesn't spend much time outside on nice days, wait until it rains: You'll be lucky to get his big toe out the door. Chow Chows hate water. Some have been known to hold it for days until it was dry enough to go outside.

As you might expect, their dislike of rain extends to all forms of water. I heard of a Chow Chow who got loose and wandered into a pond (a strange enough occurrence by itself!). Rather than swim back to shore, however, his heavy coat weighed him down and caused him to sink, so he had to be rescued. He was unable to move in the water at all.

Shoo Li's antiwater campaign may bother his owner most at bath time. Luckily he doesn't need many baths to stay clean (more on that in chapter 6), but for the first few times in the tub, ask a friend or family member to help you hold Shoo Li, and try to make bath time pleasant. Give him a piece of cheese for standing still, and be as thorough and fast as you can.

Chows and Other Living Things

Chow Chows dislike water, including baths, as you can tell by this one's expression. He's been trained to behave in the tub, but he's not too happy about getting wet.

Children As mentioned earlier, Chows bond to their families quickly and remain devoted. They are one-family dogs, carrying their devotion to all members of their family with them to the end.

Despite reports to the contrary, Chows are good with kids—when they're not expected to act like more boisterous playmates. Chow Chows assume responsibility for all members of their family and make wonderful guardians for children. Chows and children who grow up together will be the fastest of friends.

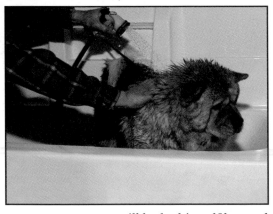

But it's up to adults to tell children what they can and cannot do to, or expect from, the family Chow. Shoo Li will not necessarily welcome Sally's friends, nor will he let himself be used as a beanbag chair or toy by strange children.

Dogs and Other Pets If Shoo Li is the newest addition to a dog-owning household, he will quickly learn the hierarchy among his canine cohorts and adjust to his place. Females tend to argue among themselves more than do males, and if you're leaving your dogs alone in the house for some time while you go out, it's a good idea to keep them separated. You can use a baby gate to divide a couple of rooms. It's nice if they can sniff and see each other, but you don't want them running to the door to bark at a stranger, only to get into a tussle on the landing.

Most Chow Chows don't get along with cats, and it's not advisable to leave Shoo Li in the same room with a free-roaming ferret, hamster, bird or other small pet.

Who's in Charge?

Shoo Li will look to his human family for kind leadership, and it's important he get it; otherwise he may decide to take matters into his own hands. It's not a good idea to let any dog do this, but to let a discerning creature like the Chow Chow dictate who's in charge of what could be disastrous.

To earn Shoo Li's respect (and, consequently, devotion), let him know who's in charge from the time you bring him home. Every once in a while, turn him over so that he's on his back and you're over him. Keep him there for a few seconds, rubbing his belly and looking non-threateningly but directly

---

A DOG'S SENSES

Sight: With their eyes located farther apart than ours, dogs can detect movement at a greater distance than we can, but they can't see as well up close. They can also see better in less light, but can't distinguish many colors.

Sound: Dogs can hear about four times better than we can, and they can hear high-pitched sounds especially well. Their ancestors, the wolves, howled to let other wolves know where they were; our dogs do the same, but they have a wider range of vocalizations, including barks, whimpers, moans and whines.

Smell: A dog's nose is his greatest sensory organ. His sense of smell is so great he can follow a trail that's weeks old, detect odors diluted to one-millionth the concentration we'd need to notice them, even sniff out a person under water!

Taste: Dogs have fewer taste buds than we do, so they're likelier to try anything—and usually do, which is why it's especially important for their owners to monitor their food intake. Dogs are omnivores, which means they eat meat as well as vegetable matter like grasses and weeds.

Touch: Dogs are social animals and love to be petted, groomed and played with.

into his eyes. Be firm when asking Shoo Li to do anything, and don't let him get away with doing something
you don't want him to continue to do as a grown dog.

Socializing and Training

Because of their reserved nature as adults, it's extremely important to socialize Chow Chows as soon as
possible after they've received all their shots.

*The key to a
well-adjusted
Chow Chow is
to socialize,
socialize,
socialize. Start
in puppyhood
and continue
throughout
your dog's life.*

Take advantage of the
puppy Chow's playful-
ness and curiosity and
take him everywhere
with you. Introduce
Shoo Li to your neigh-
bors, reminding them
to approach him at
his level and not be
rough with him. Bring
him in the car with
you, and take walks
in strange parks, over
gravel and concrete,
in a noisy town or
city. Take Shoo Li to
a puppy training class,
and for added fun
and bonding, contin-
ue with regular obedience classes. You can make or
break Shoo Li's attitude toward strange people, places
or things. So if you want a confident dog who's happy
to go exploring with you and isn't skittish about
strangers, then socialize, socialize, socialize.

A word of advice: Chow Chows are very sensitive. They
don't like harsh corrections, and they really don't need
them. They are quick learners, and though not considered "task intelligent" the way sporting, working
and some other breeds are, they strive to please and
will learn to do anything they really want to do. It's
your job to make it interesting for them.

If Shoo Li's doing something you don't want him to do, a firm and emphatic "No!" along with a reprimanding stare should do the trick. Remember, you're in charge. (More on training in chapter 8.)

Know About the Negatives

Why do people give up their Chow Chows? Most often because they are not the dogs they "expected." Before your expectations run too high and are left unmet, here are some other important things to know about this dog.

Because of their shortened muzzles, many Chow Chows **snore** at night.

Chow Chows do not like the heat or humidity, and it doesn't take much to make them pant heavily. When they do that, they tend to **drool**. In fact, because they have slightly droopy jowls, they tend to drool anyway.

Chows get along well enough with each other and other dogs, but cats and other small pets beware!

The **heat** can make a Chow Chow sick, and it takes an observant owner to notice when a situation has become an emergency. You see, Chows are stoics and are great at hiding when they're not feeling well. If you notice your dog's normally blue-black tongue turning lighter or getting splotchy in the heat, it's time to cool him off—quickly! Hose him down or apply ice packs around his groin, and get him to the veterinarian.

Coat Care

The Chow Chow's luxurious coat is his loveliest attribute—and his greatest curse for his owner. Chow Chows **shed**. Profusely. Often. Smooth Chows shed loose hairs; rough Chows shed handfuls.

They "blow coat" twice a year—in the spring and in the fall. Females sometimes more often. If you're not prepared to have hair everywhere for a few times a year, the Chow Chow is going to be hard for you to cope with. Chow Chows need regular grooming to keep the hair loss under control. You'll soon learn you have to change your vacuum cleaner bags often, and you'll need to keep an appliance for catching hair in the drain of your tub. Chows can be tough on plumbing.

Shoo Li's lovely locks also provide a great feasting and breeding ground for fleas, which love the damp warmth right by the skin. Even a couple of stray fleas on a Chow Chow can leave you with an infestation on your dog and in your home in a matter of days. It's another reason to be diligent with your grooming (in-depth information on grooming is provided in chapter 6).

Chow Chows shed and will need regular grooming— even the smooths.

On the plus side, Shoo Li's well-cared-for tresses will be a pleasure to look at and touch, and will get lots of compliments from friends and neighbors. Also, Chow Chows don't have that characteristic doggy odor when bathed on a regular basis.

SMOOTHS VS. ROUGHS

If you're getting to know Chow Chows, you need to know the differences between the smooths and the roughs. Chow Chow breeders themselves have dueled over the varieties, and smooths were written out of the breed standard for over forty years; it wasn't until the mid 1980s that they were reinstated. Smooth Chows were being shown even when they weren't officially written into the breed's standard, but now that they are "official," they're getting more consistent recognition in the showring.

The most obvious difference is the amount of hair each has, the smooth sporting a sleek coat and the rough a more bushy, flowing fur. Another cosmetic difference is in the amount of skin on their faces. Rough Chows have more pronounced wrinkles on their faces, and as a result, more limited peripheral vision.

The differences are not all cosmetic. Smooths, on the whole, are more outgoing and more even-tempered; nothing seems to faze them. And they're infinitely easier to groom. Because of their more gregarious personalities and less demanding upkeep, smooths are becoming more popular as pets. But it's still the rough who gets the most attention, and as a result there aren't many smooth Chow breeders.

CHARACTERISTICS OF THE CHOW CHOW
Independent
Dignified
Loyal
Undemanding
Neat
Dislikes rain and water
Sensitive
Sheds profusely

The Greatest Dog for the Right Owner

In sum, the Chow Chow is a proud, noble, independent dog who, once a member of your family, will love you madly—on his own terms. Extend him the simple pleasure of being around you at home and on the road, and you'll have a very happy dog and a handsome, trusted friend.

MORE INFORMATION ON CHOW CHOWS

NATIONAL BREED CLUB

The Chow Chow Club, Inc.
Irene Cartabio, Corresponding Secretary
3580 Plover Place
Seaford, NY 11783

The club can send you information on all aspects of the breed, including the names and addresses of breed clubs in your area, as well as obedience clubs. Inquire about membership.

BOOKS

Atkinson, James. *Chow Chows: A Complete Pet Owner's Manual.* Hauppauge, N.Y.: Barron's Educational Series, 1988.

Draper, Dr. Samuel and Joan McDonald Brearley. *The World of the Chow Chow.* Neptune, N.J.: TFH Publications, 1992.

Kopath, L. J. Kip. *The Complete Chow Chow.* New York: Howell Book House, 1988.

Pisano, Beverly. *Chow Chows.* Neptune, N.J.: TFH Publications, 1990.

MAGAZINES

Chow Life
The Official Publication of the Chow Chow Club
P.O. Box 1070
Chester, CA 96020

VIDEOS

American Kennel Club, *Chow Chows.*

OTHER

Society for the Preservation of Smooth Coat
Chow Chows
Lawrence Pilgrim
Rte. 3, Box 1405
Byron, GA 31008-9714

This is an off-shoot of The Chow Chow Club and was founded by Smooth Chow owners and breeders. If you'd like information just about Smooths, contact this club.

Living

with a

part two

Chow Chow

chapter 4

Bringing Your
Chow Chow
Home

The author with a puppy.

A little advance planning will help you enjoy your new Chow Chow and will keep him happy, healthy and safe.

Socializing Your Puppy

Shoo Li will remember all his life what he learns about the world when he is between seven and sixteen weeks old. Those nine weeks will shape his personality, making him steadfast or shy, dignified or aggressive, eager to learn or resentful of training.

Be diligent about Shoo Li's socialization by taking him out and about as soon as he is safely vaccinated. Good socialization includes familiarizing him with the people, animals, objects and noises he will encounter during everyday life. He should be introduced to a variety of friendly people and to gentle dogs. He should ride in cars (other than on a trip to the veterinarian); walk on varied footing such as concrete, linoleum, grass and carpet; and encounter bicycles, shopping carts, joggers and traffic sounds (all on-lead, of course). Help is available if you want it. Dog clubs and obedience schools often hold kindergarten puppy classes for socializing puppies. Find them through newspaper classifieds or the yellow pages, or ask your veterinarian.

Puppy Proofing Your Home

Until Shoo Li is housebroken and has stopped teething, confine him to one easily cleaned room of your home when there is no one home to supervise him. The kitchen or a bathroom is ideal. Basements and garages are too isolated to teach a puppy how to be part of the family. A wire mesh baby gate (not plastic or wood, which are easily chewed) often works better than a door when confining a young puppy to a room.

To make the room (and the rest of your home) safe for Shoo Li when he is unsupervised, put all cleaning agents, antifreeze, pesticides, drugs (nonprescription and prescription) and other household, garage or garden chemicals out of his reach. If it isn't possible to eliminate electrical wires that Shoo Li can reach, coat them with Bitter Apple, a safe, bad-tasting substance especially created to prevent chewing. If you have houseplants, identify them and make sure they aren't poisonous. Many common houseplants are. All plants should be placed out of Shoo Li's reach because no puppy can resist playing with a plant, but extra precautions are necessary with poisonous plants. If you like your nontoxic plants just where they are and want Shoo Li to learn to leave them alone, spray them with Bitter Apple leaf protector.

An unsupervised puppy will teethe on whatever is reachable. It's important to close cupboard doors as

PUPPY ESSENTIALS

Your new puppy will need:

food bowl

water bowl

collar

leash

I.D. tag

bed

crate

toys

grooming supplies

Shoo Li could gnaw on anything from a box of dish-washer soap to raw potatoes to brillo pads. But don't worry: Securing closet and cupboard doors or flipping the shower curtain up over the rod aren't so hard to remember once you have your precious puppy.

Your puppy will want to explore everything, so know which plants in your home may be toxic, and make sure your pup doesn't chew them.

The Great Crate

Dogs descend from denning animals that spent a great deal of their time in the relative security of their lair. That's why it will take only a brief period of adjustment before Shoo Li feels comfortable and protected in a dog crate. Contrary to being cruel, as some new dog owners imagine, dog crates have saved dogs' lives and owners' tempers.

Buy puppy Shoo Li a crate that is large enough for a grown Chow Chow to stand up and turn around in comfortably. The crate will be a tremendous help with housebreaking, because Shoo Li will soon learn not to soil his bed. It can also serve as a safe playpen so that Shoo Li can't damage furniture or swallow something dangerous when you are away or asleep. In addition, when secured in your vehicle, the crate is a life-saving doggie car seat. Shoo Li's crate should be placed in his puppy-proofed room, right up front near the baby gate.

Shoo Li's crate should be snug, soft and comfortable inside. The bedding should be easy to change and not dangerous if chewed or swallowed. For example, several thicknesses of newspaper (black and white, not color like the Sunday Comics) make good indoor bedding.

Every time you put Shoo Li in his crate, toss a favorite toy or a special treat in the crate ahead of him. Say "crate" and, as gently as possible, put your puppy in and shut the door. Shoo Li may cry the first few times he is introduced to his crate, but if you walk away and don't take him out of the crate until he settles down, he'll soon become accustomed to it.

If it's impossible to give Shoo Li his own puppy-proofed room, you can still enjoy the benefits of a crate. In fact, without a confined play area for your puppy, a crate becomes almost essential. Coming home to a safely crated puppy is much nicer for both of you than arriving home to find a messy rug and teeth marks on the furniture. (For more on training, including housetraining, see chapter 8.)

Crates are not only excellent housetraining aids, they serve as your puppy's own quiet spot in the house.

Exercise

One of the reasons Chow Chows adapt well to city life is because they need less exercise than most dogs their size. Even so, leading an active life will make Shoo Li live longer, look healthier and behave better. Brisk walks are good for both of you, and Shoo Li would also enjoy a securely fenced play area with sufficient shade and a couple of dog toys.

Sleepy Time

Young puppies tire easily and should be allowed to sleep until they wake up on their own. Even the healthiest, happiest Chow pups become limp as dishrags when it's snooze time, and naps are sudden, frequent, and often short when puppies are young. As puppies grow older, they snooze less often but stay asleep for a longer time. Teach your children that Shoo Li needs his sleep to grow big and strong the same as they do, and shouldn't be awakened when he is napping.

Puppies and dogs housebreak easier and stay healthier if they are on a regular schedule of feeding and exercise. Chapter 5 covers feeding schedules for Chow Chows of different ages.

HOUSEHOLD DANGERS

Curious puppies and inquisitive dogs get into trouble not because they are bad, but simply because they want to investigate the world around them. It's our job to protect our dogs from harmful substances, like the following:

IN THE HOUSE

cleaners, especially pine oil

perfumes, colognes, aftershaves

medications, vitamins

office and craft supplies

electric cords

chicken or turkey bones

chocolate

some house and garden plants, like ivy, oleander and poinsettia

IN THE GARAGE

antifreeze

garden supplies, like snail and slug bait, pesticides, fertilizers, mouse and rat poisons

Safe Toys

Toys are not an extra but an essential. Shoo Li needs something safe to gnaw on while he is teething and should have a couple toys available all the time. Chewing is good for dogs as it helps remove plaque from their teeth and promotes healthy gums. Shoo Li will still enjoy chewing when he grows up, though much less so. Chow Chows are not big chewers once they're past the teething stage. Still, having appropriate chew toys around will keep him from seeking out furniture or other things if the urge strikes him.

Rawhide chew toys are a traditional favorite, but there have been rare accidents when a dog ripped a chunk from a rawhide, got it caught in its throat, and choked. So, give Shoo Li rawhide only when you are home and in the same room with him, and don't choose rawhide for his crate toy.

Squeaky toys (lightweight rubber or plastic with squeakers inside) are popular with pups, but they are safe only when you are either watching or joining in the play. These types of toys are easily torn apart by Chow puppies and then swallowed, dangerous squeaker and all. Keep Shoo Li's squeaky toy out of his reach and bring it out every few days for some special minutes of fun.

Chew toys made of hard nylon are safe in Shoo Li's mouth even when you aren't at home. Puppies prefer the softer, equally safe, gummy-type nylon chews. Solid, hard rubber toys are also safe and fun, but an occasional adult dog is able to mangle even those labeled "indestructible." If you see that Shoo Li is gouging pieces out of his rubber toys, don't leave him alone with them.

Puppies need their sleep to grow big and strong.

The braided rope toys sold at pet supply stores are fun for games of tug, and good for helping to keep Shoo Li's teeth tartar free. If Shoo Li starts unstringing his rope, don't let him alone with it, as swallowing the strings could cause intestinal problems. For the ultimate puppy treat, buy a sterilized bone toy and stuff it with cheese. This crate toy will keep Shoo Li occupied for a long time.

Never give Shoo Li real bones or discarded shoes. Although he would like them, each is harmful in its own way. Real bones can splinter and damage his mouth, get stuck in his throat or tear his digestive tract. Delicious old shoes give Shoo Li an open invitation to taste your new ones; after all, dogs can't be expected to tell the difference.

45

Practical Dog Dishes

Practical dog dishes are both easy to clean and shaped or weighted so that they are difficult to tip over. Shoo Li should have one for food and another for water. The food dish should be washed after each use, and the water dish should be refilled with fresh water frequently and washed thoroughly once a day. When selecting dishes, remember that Shoo Li will grow, and so will the size of his meals.

Grooming Gizmos

Keeping Shoo Li's profuse coat in brilliant condition will take a variety of grooming implements. The basic tool for his puppy coat is a three-inch-deep Poodle

comb with widely spaced teeth for the neck and body. In addition, a one-inch-deep comb with the teeth spaced close on one side and far apart on the other is good for tackling the tangles behind the ears and lower legs, and a flea comb works best on the muzzle and lower jaw. A heavy-duty toenail clipper is also a necessity.

When Shoo Li grows up, you will need a few more grooming gizmos. For his rarely needed bath,

Your puppy will need a properly fitting collar and a leash made of leather or nylon webbing that's about six feet long. You'll have lots of styles to choose

you should have a high-quality pH-balanced (for dogs) shampoo and a coat conditioner (sometimes you may need insecticide shampoo or dip). You'll also need a slicker brush, a curved pin brush with rounded tips, a soft toothbrush and thinning shears. The rest of Shoo Li's bathing and grooming needs are probably already in your medicine chest. (See chapter 6 for complete information on grooming your Chow Chow.)

First Collar and Lead

Wait until you bring Shoo Li home before buying a collar, so you can get one that will fit his neck perfectly. The collar should apply no pressure as it encircles his neck, but it shouldn't be loose enough to slip off over his head.

Purchase a collar that is flat, made of nylon webbing or leather, with a buckle and ring for attaching the leash. Check the fit of Shoo Li's collar weekly. Puppies grow fast, and collars must be replaced immediately when they become too small. Shoo Li should never go outside without wearing his collar (and lead unless he is in a fenced area), but you may want to consider removing it when he is in the house. Even a properly fitted collar worn twenty-four hours a day will eventually damage his regal ruff.

Shoo Li's lead should be five to six feet long and made of leather, nylon webbing or some other strong flexible fabric. Another choice is a retractable lead, which gives you the option of keeping Shoo Li close to you (in traffic) or giving him up to thirty feet of freedom (in open spaces) at the touch of a button. When purchasing a retractable lead, get one in a strength that will easily control an adult Chow. Neither Shoo Li's collar nor lead should be made of chain. You may want a chain training collar as a teaching aid when Shoo Li is older, but he should wear it only for training, not in place of his regular collar.

Rope toys help remove tartar from teeth while your dog chews on them. They also make great tug toys.

Other Supplies

Available in pet supply stores, poop scoops are convenient for cleaning up your yard. It's also important to clean up after Shoo Li when you take him for walks. In many places, it's the law.

Before bringing Shoo Li home, you will want to have nutritious puppy food in the cupboard and the address and phone number of a trusted veterinarian. See chapter 5 for more on feeding and chapter 7 for more on veterinary care.

Feeding
Your
Chow Chow

Good nutrition is essential to prevent dietary deficiency diseases. It also keeps Suni energized and her coat healthy, reduces her susceptibility to organic diseases and helps ward off infections. When planning Suni's diet, remember that more is not better. Many adult Chow Chows do not have a large appetite for their size and become full rather quickly. That's why its important to provide quality, not quantity.

Puppies, on the other hand, may have a tendency to overeat. It takes a lot of willpower to pick up baby Suni's empty dish instead of giving her a second helping when she was chowing down so happily. But overfeeding Suni isn't doing her a favor. Roly-poly puppies might look cute, but extra pounds put too much stress on immature hips, spines and pasterns. This can result in pain and problems at maturity.

Why Bargain Hunting Is Bad

Bargain dog food is seldom a bargain. Even though the nutritional information on the package says it has the same amount of protein as the respected and better-known brands, what's important is the amount of usable (digestible) protein. For example, shoe leather is protein, but it has no nutritive value at all.

Once you have found a high-quality dog food that Suni thrives on, don't change brands because something else is on sale. A successful diet shouldn't be changed without a very good reason, and the new food must be introduced gradually, as sudden changes in diet can upset your dog's stomach.

Feeding Your Puppy

When you purchased Suni, the breeder probably told you which food your puppy was already used to and gave you a feeding schedule. If Suni is happy, healthy and beautiful on the feed and schedule her breeder recommended, there is no reason to change. But if you did not get a breeder recommendation, or believe Suni would do better on a different feed, choose a reputable brand of puppy food—one that has been on the market for many years—and feed it according to label directions. When changing feeds, mix the new brand with the old, increasing the amount of the new brand gradually until the changeover is complete. Make the change in the same gradual way when Suni reaches a year old and is ready for adult dog food.

> ### HOW MANY MEALS A DAY?
>
> Individual dogs vary in how much they should eat to maintain a desired body weight—not too fat, but not too thin. Puppies need several meals a day, while older dogs may need only one. Determine how much food keeps your adult dog looking and feeling her best. Then decide how many meals you want to feed with that amount. Like us, most dogs love to eat, and offering two meals a day is more enjoyable for them. If you're worried about overfeeding, make sure you measure correctly and abstain from adding tidbits to the meals.
>
> Whether you feed one or two meals, only leave your dog's food out for the amount of time it takes her to eat it—10 minutes, for example. Freefeeding (when food is available any time) and leisurely meals encourage picky eating. Don't worry if your dog doesn't finish all her dinner in the allotted time. She'll learn she should.

While Suni is growing, remember to increase the size of her meals gradually as she gets bigger. Between seven and twelve weeks of age, she will need four meals a day, and from three to five months, she should be fed three times daily. By the time she is five months old, she will probably need more than twice the amount that she ate as a three-month-old, but she doesn't have to eat as often. By then, two meals a day are sufficient. As an adult (over twelve months old), Suni will probably eat slightly less than she did as a growing puppy and will need to eat only once a day. Look at her to tell whether her food keeps her in top condition. Suni's coat should be profuse and shiny, her eyes should be bright and she should be in good, solid flesh. Whatever you do, don't allow her to become fat; many serious health problems in dogs have been traced directly to obesity.

During adolescence (five to eleven months or more of age), Suni may appear a little on the slender side when compared with a fully mature Chow, but as long as she is energetic, with a pleasant disposition and a gleaming coat, her nutritive requirements are probably being met. Poor nutrition almost always shows up first in the quality of the coat. If Suni's coat is dry or dull, consider it an early warning signal that something is wrong. Have your veterinarian examine her; it's possible that the quality and quantity of her food are fine but she might need to be wormed, or

HOW TO READ THE DOG FOOD LABEL

With so many choices on the market, how can you be sure you are feeding the right food for your dog? The information is all there on the label—if you know what you're looking for.

Look for the nutritional claim right up top. Is the food "100% nutritionally complete"? If so, it's for nearly all life stages; "growth and maintenance," on the other hand, is for early development; puppy foods are marked as such, as are foods for senior dogs.

Ingredients are listed in descending order by weight. The first three or four ingredients will tell you the bulk of what the food contains. Look for the highest-quality ingredients, like meats and grains, to be among them.

The Guaranteed Analysis tells you what levels of protein, fat, fiber and moisture are in the food, in that order. While these numbers are meaningful, they won't tell you much about the quality of the food. Nutritional value is in the dry matter, not the moisture content.

In many ways, seeing is believing. If your dog has bright eyes, a shiny coat, a good appetite and a good energy level, chances are his diet's fine. Your dog's breeder and your veterinarian are good sources of advice if you're still confused.

treated for a condition unrelated to nutrition. If her nutritional needs are not being met, your veterinarian may recommend that you change brands of dog food. Remember to do it gradually and don't expect miracles. It will be several weeks before you see a difference.

Some owners like to supplement their puppy's diet with vitamins. When you supplement, the key consideration is balance. Over-supplementation is dangerous and has been linked to a variety of ills, including hip dysplasia, and some vitamins work only in combination with the correct ratio of other vitamins. If you believe Suni would benefit from vitamins, give them according to your veterinarian's directions.

Feeding Your Adult Chow

As an adult, Suni may be fed one large meal a day, or two smaller ones if you prefer. Some breeders recommend the two smaller meals a day to help prevent the medical emergency problem of bloat, which can occur in deep-chested breeds such as the Chow (see chapter 7 for more on bloat). Dogs are creatures of habit and so are their digestive systems, so feed her at the same time every day.

When selecting Suni's adult dog food, make your first choice the adult variety of the puppy food she grew up on, and give it a three- to six-month trial. Then, if you are dissatisfied with it, ask your veterinarian or Suni's breeder for a recommendation. When you find a high-quality adult feed that Suni enjoys, there is no reason to change brands for many years provided that she feels well and looks good after six months of eating it. Dog foods are specially packaged to attract you, not your dog. Suni won't get bored with the same food every day like you would, and doesn't need to discover new shapes, colors and sizes in her bowl at frequent intervals. As long as you are feeding a respected brand and Suni is thriving, it is unlikely that any change would be for the better.

As some Chows may develop skin problems in their adult life, many breeders believe dog foods with no soy added are the best for Chows. Many owners note skin problems sometimes lessen when soy-free food is fed. This is something that will vary with each individual Chow. Consult with your veterinarian about your dog's diet if you notice skin problems or have questions about the food you're feeding.

Many adult Chows retain their proper weight consistently when fed a little extra during the winter and a little less during the heat of summer. Don't worry if Suni shows less interest in her food during the warm months; she will probably have her appetite back by November.

When Suni grows old, she may show less interest in her food for a number of reasons. One of them is sore teeth. If dental problems are causing Suni pain, your veterinarian can make feeding time a pleasure again. If age is dulling her senses, warming her food will give it a more appetizing aroma. Also, offering much smaller amounts of food several times a day, instead of one big dinner, sometimes entices an elderly dog to eat.

Older dogs do better when fed a dog food with a lower percentage of protein than they ate during their prime. The change should be made gradually, of course, and is usually easiest on the dog when you stick to the same brand but go to a formula lower in protein. Most brand-name dog foods come in several varieties, and you can easily find a variety with less protein by reading the nutrition information on the back of the bag. Some brands even make a special formula just for older dogs.

Supplements

There are special times in a dog's life when supplementing the diet may be advisable. Females who have been bred, and females nursing puppies, may need a little extra, especially if their appetites are suffering. Show dogs may be stressed from constantly traveling and competing. If you think your Chow Chow might benefit from supplementation, check with your veterinarian. He or she may suggest the addition of cottage cheese, hard-boiled (never raw) egg whites, an occasional sliver of raw beef liver or a little fat to your dog's diet, or may put her on a prepared vitamin-mineral powder or tablet.

What's in Your Dog's Dinner?

All dogs require food containing the proper proportions of digestible proteins, carbohydrates, fats, vitamins and minerals.

Protein is not stored, so your Chow Chow must receive it every day of her life. It is used for bone growth, tissue healing, maintenance of the essential supply of amino acids, and the daily replacement of body tissues burned up by normal activity.

Carbohydrates aid digestion and elimination, provide energy and help assure the proper assimilation of fats. Excess carbohydrates are stored in the body for future use.

Fats are necessary as an energy source and to add shine to Suni's coat and suppleness to her skin. But excess fats are stored under the skin and can result in an overweight dog. The fat balance is important. Too much leads to the same obesity problems that humans suffer from, while too little could contribute to coat and skin problems, insufficient insulation and lack of energy.

A high-quality dog food should supply all the nutrients your Chow needs.

Vitamin A is necessary for a healthy, shiny coat because it is used by the dog's body for fat absorption. It is also essential for normal growth rate, reproduction and good eyesight.

The **B vitamins** protect the nervous system and are also mandatory for normal coat, skin, appetite, growth and eyes.

*You'll know
your Chow's
eating right if
her coat is thick
and full, her
eyes are shiny,
and she's feel-
ing good, like
this Chow on
an agility
course obstacle.*

Dogs synthesize **vitamin C** in their own livers so it usually isn't mentioned in an analysis of commercial dog food or vitamin preparations. Some breeders add it anyway, believing that it aids healing in the event of injury, helps to prevent hip dysplasia and fights bacterial infections.

Healthy bones, teeth and muscle tone are all dependent upon **vitamin D**, but the vitamin must be taken in the correct ratio with calcium and phosphorus to be effective.

Vitamin E is associated with the proper functioning of the muscles and the internal and reproductive organs.

Vitamin K is essential to normal clotting of blood. Most dogs are able to synthesize Vitamin K in their digestive tract. If your dog seems to bleed to much and too long from a minor cut, mention it to your veterinarian. It could indicate a lack of vitamin K or a more serious problem.

Calcium and **phosphorus** must not only be present but in the correct ratio to provide puppies with protection from rickets, bowed legs and other bone deformities. They also aid muscle development and maintenance, as well as lactation in nursing bitches.

Potassium is needed for normal growth and healthy nerves and muscles.

Sodium and **chlorine** help your Chow Chow's appetite and allow her to enjoy a normal activity level. **Magnesium** is necessary to prevent convulsions and problems with the nervous system. **Iron** is needed for the healthy blood that prevents fatigue from anemia. **Iodine** prevents goiter in dogs as it does in humans. **Copper** is necessary for growing and maintaining strong bones and, like iron, helps prevent anemia. **Cobalt** aids normal growth and keeps the reproductive tract healthy. **Manganese** also aids growth and is utilized in reproduction. **Zinc** is involved in normal growth and is also an aid to healthy skin.

Commercial Dog Food

Most commercially prepared dog foods are balanced to provide your Chow with optimal nutrition and are far healthier than anything you could create at home for twice the price. As you can surmise from just the very basic information provided here, the proper balance of vitamins and minerals, fats and proteins, is too complicated and too important to guess at, and is better left to the test kitchens of the major dog food companies. Another danger is our human tendency to think that if some of a substance is good for bones or appetite or nerves, then a lot will probably be better. This is definitely not true, and in some cases, more is actually toxic.

> ## TO SUPPLEMENT OR NOT TO SUPPLEMENT?
>
> If you're feeding your dog a diet that's correct for her developmental stage and she's alert, healthy-looking and neither over- nor underweight, you don't need to add supplements. These include table scraps as well as vitamins and minerals. In fact, a growing puppy is in danger of developing musculoskeletal disorders by oversupplementation. If you have any concerns about the nutritional quality of the food you're feeding, discuss them with your veterinarian.

TYPES OF FOODS

Commercial dog foods fall into three major categories: canned, dry and semimoist.

Dry dog foods come in a variety of shapes and sizes. Some of them are in meal form, which means the ingredients are simply mixed together. Biscuit food is formed by adding flour to the dry ingredients and baking the mixture. It may be made up of whole biscuits or crumbled biscuits. Pelleted feeds are actually meal-type food pressed into pellet form.

It's important to read the label on any dry food you buy to learn how much warm water it should soak in before feeding. Some dry foods form gravy when moistened, and others simply soften and expand. Are dry foods good for your dog? Many Chow Chows have been fed dry food exclusively and lived healthy, active lives. Another popular and wholesome way to feed is to use two-thirds dry (moistened with water) and one-third canned food mixed together.

If you are planning to use only canned food, it is important to read the label carefully. Some canned foods provide total nutrition while others are formulated to be mixed with dry food. If the canned food is meant to be fed alone, it will say something like "100% complete" or "complete dinner" on the label. Some canned dinners are available either "chopped" or "chunky." The nutritional values are equal, but most puppies find it easier to eat the chopped variety, whereas adult Chow Chows often prefer their food "chunky."

Semimoist food, while convenient to use (it comes prepackaged) and less expensive than the better-quality canned foods, sometimes has a high content of salt, sugar and preservatives, so compare labels carefully. Although tempting because of the simplicity to feed, you can enjoy the same ease by portion-packing high-quality dry food in self-sealing baggies.

In addition to her regular dinner, Suni would probably enjoy an occasional dog biscuit. These hard treats help clean dogs' teeth and stimulate the gums. So that you don't

TYPES OF FOODS/TREATS

There are three types of commercially available dog food—dry, canned and semimoist—and a huge assortment of treats (lucky dogs!) to feed your dog. Which should you choose?

Dry and canned foods contain similar ingredients. The primary difference between them is their moisture content. The moisture is not just water. It's blood and broth, too, the very things that dogs adore. So while canned food is more palatable, dry food is more economical, convenient and effective in controlling tartar buildup. Most owners feed a 25% canned/75% dry diet to give their dogs the benefit of both. Just be sure your dog is getting the nutrition he needs (you and your veterinarian can determine this).

Semimoist foods have the flavor dogs love and the convenience owners want. However, they tend to contain excessive amounts of artificial colors and preservatives.

Dog treats come in every size, shape and flavor imaginable, from organic cookies shaped like postmen to beefy chew sticks. Dogs seem to love them all, so enjoy the variety. Just be sure not to overindulge your dog. Factor treats into her regular meal sizes.

overfeed your dog, consider any biscuits to be part of the total food she gets in a day.

Feeding Away from Home

Take along your dog's regular food and water from home when you go on a long outing or on vacation with your Chow Chow. In an unfamiliar area, you may have difficulty finding the same food that your dog is accustomed to, and an abrupt change of diet frequently gives dogs enough stomach trouble to spoil your vacation. It's also a good idea to take along water from home. Although strange water doesn't sicken dogs as easily as strange food does, the chemicals added in various locales may give the water an unfamiliar odor.

Some dogs seem to distrust such water and either refuse it entirely or don't drink enough of it. If you didn't bring water from home and your dog refuses to drink, buy enough bottled water for one day. At the same time, put a couple of quarts of the local water in a wide-mouth container and allow it to sit for twenty-four hours before giving it to your dog. Usually that allows the odor to dissipate enough so that your dog will drink it.

Dog-Feeding Don'ts

Don't feed your Chow Chow chocolate or any highly spiced or greasy, salty foods. Chocolate is deadly to some dogs, and spicy sauces and junk food lead to stomach upsets.

Don't believe ads that encourage you to vary your dog's diet. Dogs do best when they are fed the same brand of food daily at a regular hour. If you must add something to Suni's food, stir in a few tablespoons of a high-quality canned dog food or some cottage cheese or hard-boiled egg white. Chopped bits of fresh or cooked vegetables in small portions are also good for Suni. Just be aware that if you begin adding little extras Suni may come to expect them and go on a hunger strike when they are not available.

Don't fill Suni up with table scraps, especially when she is young. Puppies can't hold much food at a time, and no matter how nutritious your dinner is for humans, chances are your Chow's own chow is better for her. Also, dogs who eat table scraps often lose their taste for dog food completely. It's especially important not to feed Suni directly from the table. Dogs fed during dinner become accomplished beggars and are soon a major nuisance at mealtimes.

Don't give your Chow Chow any bones other than cooked knuckle bones. Chicken, turkey or pork chop bones, for example, can shatter and slice open her intestines with their sharp points, and fish bones are just as dangerous for dogs as they are for people.

Don't leave Suni's food dish down for longer than ten minutes. If she hasn't finished her food by then, remove it until the next feeding. That helps her learn to eat when and what she is fed.

Cleaning Chores

Suni's food and water dishes must be kept clean. Wash them daily to prevent the growth of disease-producing bacteria and other dangerous microorganisms. Also, her play area should be frequently cleaned up with a poop scoop, as this will help control worms and biting insects (more on those in chapter 7).

chapter 6

Grooming
Your
Chow Chow

Grooming your Chow Chow will soon become a pleasant, relaxing part of your daily routine. Daily care will keep Suni clean and shiny, but you will accomplish much more than that. Grooming feels good to you and your dog and will strengthen the bond between you. It will also save you money. Inspecting Suni for external parasites, minor injuries and early signs of skin disease while grooming helps you find and solve small problems before they become big, expensive ones.

A Good Start

There are few jobs more difficult than trimming the nails of a full-grown Chow who isn't accustomed to having her feet touched. But if

**GROOMING
TOOLS**

pin brush

slicker brush

flea comb

towel

mat rake

grooming
glove

scissors

nail
clippers

teeth-
cleaning
equipment

shampoo

conditioner

clippers

you condition Suni from puppyhood to accept grooming as a regular part of life, she will soon learn that being handled and brushed is both pleasant and serious. Pleasant because it feels so good. Serious because she is expected to behave. If Suni becomes fidgety about being handled on any part of her body, tell her "NO" sharply and firmly. By the time she is half grown, she should be steady and cooperative when you groom her.

Although you can groom Suni while she is standing quietly on the floor, the job is much easier on your back, and less tiring for your puppy, if she is lying down on her side on a sturdy (not wobbly) table with a non-slip surface. Rubber or carpet make good footing. You can purchase a table built especially for this purpose, or make a perfectly good table yourself.

Good Grooming Manners

Teach Suni to lie still on the grooming table by placing her on it, then giving her a bear hug with one of your arms going around her chest while the other goes around her buttocks. From this hugging position, pull her body toward you, and, with her legs leading the way, slide her off her feet and deposit her on her side gently but firmly. Slide your arms out from under Suni and reassure her by petting and stroking, using enough pressure to keep her in place. After petting her on one side for a couple of minutes, repeat the entire procedure and pet her on the other side. Praise Suni when she is cooperative and handle her with quiet persistence when she isn't, and in a few days she will be used to lying down for petting. After that, she should be a cinch to groom. No matter how well Suni behaves on the table, never turn your back on her while she is on it, not even when she is a grown-up. If she decided to jump or accidentally fell, she could be seriously hurt.

Groom baby Suni's body with a Poodle comb (a metal comb with widely spaced, three-inch-long teeth), and make your strokes short, but deep. In other words, don't try to comb very much hair per stroke, but start your stroke all the way down at the skin.

Combing Out

With your puppy lying on her side, begin by gently parting the hair on top of her shoulders. Use one hand to hold the rest of the coat back and your other hand to comb the hair in front of the part forward. Work toward the hand holding the hair, combing the hair forward in the direction of Suni's head. The hand holding the hair should slowly slide back in the direction of Suni's tail, releasing the next section of hair as you continue combing. Continue combing each section of hair forward, and work your way all the way back to Suni's rump as well as down across her rib cage. When you are satisfied that there are no tangles on that side of Suni's body, start on her legs. You should comb them downward, using both hands as before. Finish the first side by combing out the top and side of Suni's mane. Then turn her over and repeat the process on the other side.

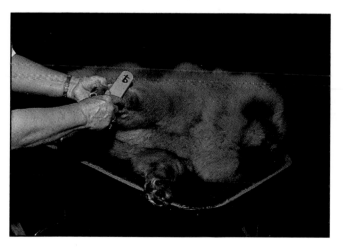

Using a grooming table will be easier on you and your Chow. Teach your dog to lie down while he's being groomed.

When you finish both sides, place Suni in a sitting position and comb out her woolly chest. Start between her legs and work upward by pushing the hair up toward her throat with one hand while you comb downward with the other. Continue all the way up to the mane.

To make the mane appear even fluffier, comb it down-ward first, then outward.

Now place Suni in a standing position to finish her legs. Stand behind her and comb the hair at the bottom of her rear legs downward. Then push the long upper rear leg hair upward with one hand while comb-ing it downward in sections as you did with the body hair. Start low and work your way up on each leg. If you want to make the upper rear leg hair appear fluffier, comb it outward after you comb it downward. Now do each front leg in the same manner.

Regular brush-ing will keep your Chow look-ing his best. It will also help you notice any skin problems or other ailments before they get out of hand.

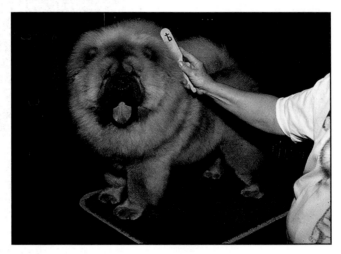

To comb Suni's tail, start at the base (part nearest the body). Hold the tail up with one hand and comb it down all the way around with the other. When you have combed it out section by section, all the way from the base to the tip, lay the tail on top of Suni's back and fan the hair forward.

Now change combs to do Suni's head. Your one-inch comb will work well on her skull. Comb forward and down gently to bring out Suni's best scowl. Now care-fully comb the fine hairs behind her ears. Be careful there for two reasons: This is one of the first areas to mat and tangle, and it's also quite sensitive. For the finishing touches, use your flea comb to remove any dead hair from Suni's muzzle and bottom jaw. Then use your one-inch comb to make Suni's mane frame her face.

In time you will become proficient in grooming, but you may feel a bit clumsy at first. Don't worry, you'll do fine. There is only one really crucial thing to remember and that is to groom Suni all the way down to the skin. If you comb only the top layer, Suni's coat will soon be seriously matted.

Brushing the Adult Chow

Once Suni's puppy fluff is replaced by a gleaming adult coat, put away your Poodle comb and replace it with brushes. Daily brushing will make Suni sparkle because brushing removes dander, dirt and dead hair while stimulating the secretion of natural oils that keep her coat healthy and shiny. It also keeps her coat from matting. Two types of brushes will be effective on Suni. The first (and the one you will use most often) is the curved pin brush with rounded tips; this brush separates the coat and removes loose hair. A slicker brush will also be useful, as it is effective for breaking up the mat you may have missed yesterday. A note of caution: Sometimes a slicker brush, if used constantly as your only brush, can break off the adult coat. It is best to use a slicker sparingly and in conjunction with a pin brush and comb.

When brushing Suni's adult coat, use two hands and part the hair just as you did when combing the puppy coat. Parting the hair ensures that you brush out Suni all the way down to the skin; anything less is absolutely useless. You should still use your flea comb and your one-inch comb to groom Suni's face, just as you did when she was a pup.

Instead of grooming Suni's adult coat daily, try every other day. If that presents no matting problem, try twice a week. Many adult Chow Chows are groomed only twice a week and almost never have a mat or a skin problem. But consider twice weekly a minimum and don't even consider grooming any less frequently than that.

Inspect Suni while brushing her. Look for open wounds that need washing and treatment, signs of skin disease, external parasites, and bumps, warts, splinters or anything else that could signal the start of a problem. Remember that ticks sometimes hide between the toes, in the ears or in the thickest part of your Chow Chow's coat (usually the neck and rump area). As you separate Suni's hair for grooming, look for fleas. Even if you don't see any, tiny dark specks are evidence that your dog is being used as a bed-and-breakfast. Ask your veterinarian to recommend preparations to rid Suni (and your home) of external parasites, and use the insecticide formulas exactly as advised on their labels.

Teeth and Toenails

To check Suni's teeth for tartar, hold her head firmly and lift her lips upward. A soft toothbrush or damp washcloth dipped in baking soda usually removes discolorations on the teeth. If the stains are not easily removed, ask your veterinarian whether Suni's teeth need a professional cleaning. Hard dog biscuits and nylon chew toys will help keep a young dog's teeth white but aren't always enough to do the whole job.

Suni's toenails are too long if they make clicking noises on the floor when she walks or touch the ground when she is standing still. Dogs with very long nails tend to walk on the back of their feet, leading to splayed toes and an unattractive gait. Not only is this uncomfortable for the dog, but there is an additional danger: If untrimmed, toenails and dewclaws eventually curl under the foot, circling back to puncture the pads. This problem doesn't occur in wolves, coyotes or even stray dogs, because in their quest for food, they cover enough ground to wear their toenails down to a practical length.

To clip Suni's nails, lift her foot up and forward; then hold it securely in your left hand so that your right hand can do the trimming (reverse this procedure if you are left-handed). If Suni has light-colored nails, your job is easier than if her nails are dark. There is a blood vessel called the quick in the bottom stem of the nail, which is clearly seen through light nails. Trim the nail just outside the quick. You won't be able to see the quick in dark nails, so make the cut just outside the hooklike projection on the underside of the nail.

When you cut the nail properly, Suni will feel nothing more than slight pressure, the same as you feel when cutting your own toenails. If you accidentally cut the quick, Suni's nail will hurt and bleed. Stop the bleeding with a styptic pencil made for human use, or use the styptic powder sold at pet supply stores. Pressing the bleeding nail into a soft bar of soap for a minute or so will also stop the bleeding. Try to work under good lighting so that you can cut Suni's nails without a mishap. Suni will forgive a cut quick if it is a rare occurrence, but if you are clumsy too often, she may begin to resist work on her feet.

Nail care is a difficult, but necessary, job. This Chow's getting extra attention and having his nails grinded after trimming.

Many owners prefer to use an electric or battery-powered nail grinder. Although you will need to acquaint your Chow with the noise of its motor, a grinder is a safe way to keep those nails short with less chance for accidental bleeding. Grinders can be purchased at many pet stores or through pet supply catalogs.

Bath Time

Since brushing cleans the coat and reduces body odors, Suni will rarely need a bath if she is thoroughly and regularly brushed. Bathe her only when necessary, because shampooing dries the coat by washing away natural oils.

Equipment for a bath includes old clothes (when Suni shakes, you'll be as wet as she is); a tub, preferably with a drain so that Suni won't be standing in soapy water; a rubber mat for traction in the tub; a spray-nozzle hose attachment; pH-balanced dog shampoo or insecticide shampoo (and a flea and tick dip, if necessary); coat conditioner; cotton balls; two washcloths; mineral oil; several large towels; and a blow-dryer.

Before bathing Suni, allow her to exercise outside for a few minutes. That way she won't have to dash outdoors to go potty (and probably roll in the loose garden dirt) immediately following her bath. You should also brush her out thoroughly before her bath.

Luckily, Chows don't need baths very often, but when they do, make sure you have your supplies on hand.

Suni's bath water should be warm, but not hot. Begin by placing cotton balls inside each of her ears, to keep the water out. Next, spray water over Suni's whole body with the exception of her face and head. Put a small amount of shampoo on her back and massage the lather well into her coat.

Getting water or shampoo all the way through the undercoat to a Chow's skin can be difficult, but using a washcloth to rub the shampoo deeply through the coat is a big help. Add more shampoo as needed to clean her legs, neck, tail and underbelly. If you accidentally get soap in Suni's eyes, put a few drops of mineral oil in the inner corner of each eye to relieve the sting. Use the hose to rinse off the lather; then soap her up again. Now rinse thoroughly, and whatever you do, don't rush this step. Shampoo left to dry in the coat makes it dull and can cause intense itching. Use coat conditioner as per label directions. If you are using insecticide shampoo or dip on your veterinarian's recommendation, follow the label directions carefully.

Finish by wiping Suni's face and head with a warm, well-wrung washcloth. Remove the cotton from her ears and wipe them out with a dry cotton ball dipped in a bit of mineral oil. Then wrap Suni in a towel, lift her from the tub, and blot her well with several towels.

You may think Suni is dry when she is still quite damp where it counts—near the skin. A Chow's topcoat dries rather quickly, but her undercoat retains moisture. Be especially careful to dry Suni well behind the ears, on her tail and the top of the back where the tail lays, on the chest and belly, the elbow and "underarm" area, and around the genital region.

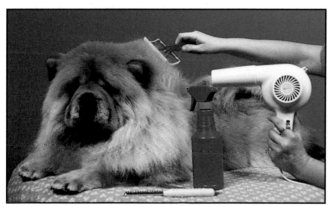

Soak up as much water as you can with towels before proceeding with blow-drying your Chow.

Use a blow-dryer after you have thoroughly blotted Suni's coat with towels, removing as much water as possible for her coat. Brush while you are blowing, and keep the dryer on high speed but cool heat. When Suni is dry, walk her on-lead so that she can relieve herself. Allowing her to frisk in the yard by herself immediately following a bath is the same as giving her an invitation to roll in the dirt. A few hours after the bath, her coat will feel natural to her once again and she will be less inclined to roll.

An Important No-No

During hot summers, well-meaning people sometimes take pity on a profusely coated dog like the Chow Chow and suggest that the dog would be happier if she had a haircut or were clipped. Don't believe it!

Clipping Suni will make her extremely uncomfortable because her double coat provides insulation from extremes of heat and cold. She prefers cold to heat, however, and must always be provided with a shady spot when she is outdoors.

Someday, due to travel or illness, you may neglect Suni's coat for an extended period of time and it may become seriously matted. Even then, do not have her clipped. If you are unable to remove the mats with your fingers or your grooming implements (along with a liquid detangling solution), take her to a grooming salon. Tell the professionals that you want the mats removed, but as much of the coat saved as possible.

The Inside-Outs of Good Looks

Good grooming is no substitute for poor health or lack of physical fitness. Good looks start from within, with quality food, regular exercise, clean housing and no internal or external parasites. Health problems sometimes show themselves first through a dry brittle coat, lacking in luster. Chow Chows in good condition sparkle from the inside out. Their regular grooming sessions help them stay healthy and bring the wholesome glow to the surface.

chapter 7

Keeping Your
Chow Chow
Healthy

When your Chow Chow is not feeling well, it's up to you to take care of him. Like people, dogs become ill with certain diseases, but with an eye on prevention and by providing him with regular care and attention, you will find that the times when your Chow Chow is really sick will be infrequent. If you learn to recognize when your Chow's not feeling his best, you can keep minor problems from escalating into major ones.

This chapter will start you off with preventive care information, then explore common ailments and progress to more serious problems, including diseases to which your Chow Chow is particularly prone.

69

Preventive Care

The easiest way to make sure your dog is well cared for is to establish a routine, then follow it every day.

For optimal health, your Chow Chow needs high-quality dog food (see chapter 6), fresh clean water, exercise and sleep (see chapter 4). He needs these every day, in varying amounts as he grows older. Beyond this basic care, *take the time, every day, to run your hands over your Chow Chow.* You can do this while you're grooming him. But don't just pet and brush him; instead, run your fingers through and under the coat so that you can feel the dog's skin. As you do this, you will get to know the feel of your dog. Should he pick up a tick, you will feel it with your fingers. If he has a cut, a lump or bruise or a skin rash, you will feel it.

By checking the dog like this every day, you will find these things before they turn into bigger problems. When you start this routine in puppyhood, your dog will come to love it, and he will be more accepting of being petted by other people—especially the veterinarian—as an adult.

The best time for this exam is after you have brushed your Chow Chow. Start at your dog's head and, using your fingertips to navigate through the fur, feel all over your dog's head, including around his muzzle, eyes, ears and neck. Take your time and be gentle; think of it as giving your dog a massage.

Continue working your hands down your Chow's body, examining his shoulders, back, sides, legs and tail. Run your hands down each leg, handling each toe on each paw, checking for burrs and foxtails, cuts and scratches. If you find any minor cuts and scrapes, you

---

YOUR PUPPY'S VACCINES

Vaccines are given to prevent your dog from getting an infectious disease like canine distemper or rabies. Vaccines are the ultimate preventive medicine: they're given before your dog ever gets the disease so as to protect him from the disease. That's why it is necessary for your dog to be vaccinated routinely. Puppy vaccines start at eight weeks of age for the five-in-one DHLPP vaccine and are given every three to four weeks until the puppy is sixteen months old. Your veterinarian will put your puppy on a proper schedule and will remind you when to bring in your dog for shots.

can wash them off with soap and water and apply a mild antibiotic ointment. However, if a cut is gaping or looks red and inflamed, call your veterinarian. Check your Chow's tummy, too. Fleas like to hide in the groin area and behind elbows—don't miss those spots.

Once you've gone over his entire body this way, return to his head. It's time to check your Chow Chow's **mouth**, looking for inflamed gums, foreign objects or possible cracked or broken teeth. Become familiar with what the teeth look like, inside and out. This is a good time to brush the teeth, as discussed in chapter 6.

Next, clean the inside of the **ears**, gently wiping them with cotton balls moistened with witch hazel or a commercial product made especially for cleaning the ears. As you wipe out the ear, check for scratches or foreign objects and give the ear a sniff. If there is quite a bit of discharge and the ear has a sour smell, call your veterinarian; your dog may have an ear infection.

Check your Chow's **nails**. As discussed in chapter 6, they need regular trimming, but not every day. A daily check, however, will keep you posted on whether any nails are chipped or cracked.

Choosing a Veterinarian

Another excellent preventive care measure you can take with your Chow Chow is to find the right veterinarian for him and for you. Your Chow Chow's veterinarian should be someone who understands the breed and is not intimidated or overly judgmental about it.

Your Chow's veterinarian should be someone with whom you feel comfortable asking questions, who takes the time to explain things, who lets you know how emergency or after-hour situations are handled by the office, and of whose competence you're assured. If possible, get a recommendation from your puppy's breeder. If that's not possible, ask local veterinarians about their experiences with Chow Chows and interview them over the phone before scheduling a visit.

Vaccines

Vaccines are another aspect of preventive care. If given at the correct ages, vaccines will protect your Chow from some potentially life-threatening infectious diseases. These are diseases caused by bacteria, viruses, protozoa, fungi and rickettsia. Young puppies are especially susceptible. Your Chow Chow may have already received some of his shots before you brought him home. Keep him on the vaccination schedule your breeder and/or veterinarian prescribed.

Infectious diseases include distemper, infectious hepatitis, leptospirosis, parvovirus, coronavirus, parainfluenza (kennel cough) and rabies.

Distemper Distemper is a very contagious viral disease that used to kill thousands of dogs. Today's vaccines are extremely effective, but dogs still die from it.

If your Chow has an immune-system problem, or if he wasn't properly vaccinated as a puppy, he could get distemper. Symptoms show as weakness and depression, a fever and a discharge from the eyes and nose. Infected dogs cough, vomit and have diarrhea. Intravenous fluids and antibiotics may help support an infected dog, but unfortunately, most die.

Infectious Hepatitis This is a highly contagious virus that primarily attacks the liver but can also cause severe kidney damage. It is not related to the form of hepatitis that affects people. The virus is spread through contaminated saliva, mucus, urine or feces. Initial symptoms include depression, vomiting, abdominal pain, high fever and jaundice. Mild cases may be treated with intravenous fluids, antibiotics and even blood transfusions; however, the mortality rate is very high.

Leptospirosis Leptospirosis is a bacterial disease spread by the urine of infected wildlife. If your Chow Chow drinks from a contaminated stream or sniffs at a bush that has been urinated on by an infected animal, it may pick up the bacteria. The bacteria attacks the kidneys, causing kidney failure. Symptoms include fever, loss of appetite, possible diarrhea and jaundice. Antibiotics can be used to treat the disease, but the outcome is usually not good, due to the serious kidney and liver damage caused by the bacteria. Leptospirosis is highly contagious; other dogs, animals and people are susceptible.

Parvovirus Parvovirus, or parvo as it is commonly known, attacks the inner lining of the intestines, causing bloody diarrhea that has a distinct odor. It is a terrible killer of puppies and is extremely contagious. In puppies under ten weeks of age, the virus also attacks the heart, causing death, often with no other symptoms. The virus moves rapidly, and dehydration can lead to shock and death in a matter of hours.

Make sure your puppy gets all his shots at the right times, and have him neutered, too. These are both preventive measures that will keep your Chow in top health all his life.

Coronavirus As is implied by the name, this is also a virus. Coronavirus is rarely fatal to adult dogs, although it is frequently fatal to puppies. The symptoms include vomiting, loss of appetite and a yellowish, watery stool that might contain mucus or blood. The stools carry the shed virus, which is highly contagious.

Parainfluenza (Kennel Cough) This respiratory infection can be caused by any number of different viral or bacterial agents. These highly contagious, airborne agents can cause a variety of symptoms, including inflammation of the trachea, bronchi and lungs, as well as mild to severe coughing. Antibiotics may be prescribed to combat or prevent pneumonia, and a cough suppressant may quiet the cough. Luckily, the disease is usually mild and many dogs recover quickly without any treatment at all.

Rabies Rabies is a highly infectious virus usually carried by wildlife, especially bats, raccoons and skunks. Any warm-blooded animal, including humans, can be infected. The virus is transmitted through the saliva, through a bite or break in the skin. It then travels up to the brain and spinal cord and throughout the body. Behavior changes are the first sign of the disease. Animals usually seen only at night will come out during the day; fearful or shy animals will become bold and aggressive or friendly and affectionate. As the virus spreads, the animal will have trouble swallowing and will drool or salivate excessively. Paralysis and convulsions follow.

There are vaccines to combat all these diseases, and they're most effective when given at the right times and boostered regularly by your veterinarian.

Unfortunately, vaccinations are no guarantee that your Chow Chow will not get sick. Many factors determine how well a dog reacts to a vaccination, including the antibodies he got from his mother, how his own immune system reacts to the vaccine, and the dog's general state of health.

Spaying and Neutering

One of the best preventive medicines you can give your Chow Chow is a spay or neuter operation. The spay operation is for females, and removes her uterus, tubes and ovaries. When a male dog is neutered (castrated), his testicles are removed.

The only reason not to spay or neuter your dog is if the puppy is of show quality and you intend to show him or her. If you bought your puppy from a breeder, that person will probably have sold you your dog with a contract. Depending on the breeder's assessment of your puppy, the contract will either obligate you to spay or neuter the dog by a certain age or show the dog by a certain age. If the latter is the case and for some reason the dog cannot or will not be shown, then the breeder and owner can discuss spaying or neutering the dog.

WHY YOU SHOULD NOT BREED YOUR DOG

Spaying or neutering your Chow Chow will prevent her or him from reproducing. Many people breed, or want to breed, their dogs for the wrong reasons. One of the most common is that they love their pet and want to have a puppy just like him or her.
Unfortunately, a puppy from their treasured pet will not be the same. The genetic combination that created their pet was from that pet's ancestors. A puppy will be from that pet *and* from the dog to which they breed the pet. If you want a dog very much like the one you have, go back to the breeder from whom you got your dog and get another from the same lineage.

Many people feel their dog should be allowed to reproduce because he is a purebred or because he has "papers." This, however, is no assurance of quality. If you're not showing or interested in showing, you probably have a pet-quality dog. A wonderful dog, I'm sure, but not one who should necessarily be bred. Discuss this matter with a breeder if you feel strongly about breeding your Chow.

Another reason people give for wanting to breed their dogs is so that their children can see the miracle of birth. This "miracle" usually comes late at night or very early in the morning, when the kids are asleep. It can also be a heartbreaking miracle if anything goes wrong, and there is plenty that can go wrong.

ADVANTAGES OF SPAY/NEUTER

The greatest advantage of spaying (for females) or neutering (for males) your dog is that you are guaranteed your dog will not produce puppies. There are too many puppies already available for too few homes. There are other advantages as well.

ADVANTAGES OF SPAYING

No messy heats.

No "suitors" howling at your windows or waiting in your yard.

Decreased incidences of pyometra (disease of the uterus) and breast cancer.

ADVANTAGES OF NEUTERING

Lessens male aggressive and territorial behaviors, but doesn't affect the dog's personality. Behaviors are often owner-induced, so neutering is not the only answer, but it is a good start.

Prevents the need to roam in search of bitches in season.

Decreased incidences of urogenital diseases.

THE BENEFITS OF SPAY/NEUTER

The health benefits of spaying and neutering are numerous. Researchers have found that spayed and neutered dogs have less incidence of cancer later in life—up to 90 percent less. That alone is incredible. In addition, the lessened hormone drive in both males and females makes them much better companions. Spaying and neutering serves other purposes as well. A male dog who has been neutered (castrated) is less likely to roam, is less likely to show aggression toward other dogs and is less likely to urinate to mark territory. A female dog in season (receptive to males) will attract hordes of male dogs who wish to breed with her; a spayed female dog will not, of course, go through that heat season.

Common Problems

This section will cover the ailments to which all dogs are prone: fleas, ticks, worms and so on. If you have specific questions or concerns, consult your veterinarian.

EXTERNAL PARASITES

Fleas   A flea is a tiny insect about the size of a pinhead that lives by biting its host and eating its blood. It is crescent shaped, has six legs and is a tremendous jumper.

The flea is a die-hard pest.

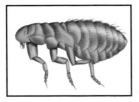

You'll know your Chow Chow has fleas if, during your daily inspection of his skin, you see a tiny darting speck trying to hide in his fur. Fleas best show up on the dog's belly, near the genitals. If you brush your Chow vigorously and you see little black specks falling to the ground, your dog has fleas. Those specks are "flea dirt," the digested, excreted blood produced by the fleas.

Fleas are extremely annoying because they cause your dog a lot of misery and they're hard to get rid of. But more than that, they're a serious health hazard. A heavy infestation can actually kill a dog, especially very young and very old dogs. Keep in mind that each time a flea bites, it eats a drop or two of blood. Multiply that by numerous bites a day times the number of fleas and you can see how dangerous an infestation can be.

Fleas, biting their host, can also cause other problems. Many Chow Chows are allergic to the flea's saliva and scratch each bite until a sore develops. This flea allergy dermatitis is a serious problem in many areas of the country. Fleas can also carry disease, such as the infamous bubonic plague, and are the intermediary host for tapeworms, an internal parasite.

Treating Fleas To reduce the flea population, you need to treat the dog *and his environment,* including inside and outside the house. If you treat only the dog and do not treat the house, yard and car, your Chow Chow will simply become reinfected. Flea eggs can live for years in the right environment, just waiting for the chance to rehatch. That's why it's so important to rid your dog and your home and car of them.

There are a number of flea-killing products on the market, including both strong chemical insecticides and natural botanical products. There is also a new medication available you can give your pet once a month that kills fleas after they bite your dog but is not harmful to the dog; ask your veterinarian about it.

FIGHTING FLEAS

Remember, the fleas you see on your dog are only part of the problem—the smallest part! To rid your dog and home of fleas, you need to treat your dog *and* your home. Here's how:

• Identify where your pet(s) sleep. These are "hot spots."

• Clean your pets' bedding regularly by vacuuming and washing.

• Spray "hot spots" with a nontoxic, long-lasting flea larvicide.

• Treat outdoor "hot spots" with insecticide.

• Kill eggs on pets with a product containing insect growth regulators (IGRs).

• Kill fleas on pets per your veterinarian's recommendation.

What you decide to use depends upon how bad your flea infestation is and your personal preferences. The stronger chemicals, such as organophosphates and carbamates, will kill the fleas, of course, but they can also kill birds and wildlife. You must read the directions and use them properly.

The natural products are not as strong, and some do not kill the flea immediately; sometimes it takes a few hours. Some products use silica or diatonaceous earth to cut or erode the flea's shell so that it dehydrates. There are also commercial products that use natural oils, such as pennyroyal, eucalyptus or citrus to repel the fleas. Use these products according to directions, as even natural products can be harmful when used incorrectly.

If you have any questions about what is safe to use on your dog, call your veterinarian or groomer. If you have questions as to how to use a particular product, call the manufacturer, who will be more than willing to talk to you and explain exactly how the product should be used.

Ticks There are several varieties of ticks in the United States, the brown dog tick being the most common. This tick is slightly larger than a sesame seed when not engorged with blood. Ticks, like fleas, live off warm-blooded host animals by sucking their blood. Ticks can carry a number of diseases, including Lyme disease (discussed below), Rocky Mountain Spotted Fever and a number of others, all of which can be very serious.

Three types of ticks (l-r): the wood tick, brown dog tick and deer tick.

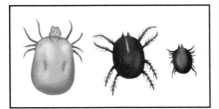

Check for ticks while you examine your Chow Chow. Ticks seem to prefer to lodge in the ears or in the hair at the base of the ear, the armpits or around the genitals. If you find a tick, smear it thoroughly with vaseline or dab it with hydrogen peroxide. As the tick suffocates in the vaseline or is stunned by the peroxide, remove it with tweezers and kill it. Don't try to kill it between your fingers, as it may get blood on you and put you at risk of becoming infected or infecting another animal. To kill a tick, put it into a sealed container of alcohol or burn it with a match.

Also, don't just grab and pull or the tick's head may separate from the body. If the head remains in the skin, an infection or abscess may result and veterinary treatment may be required. A good method for removing ticks (and fleas) is to spray or dab on a flea- or tick-killing product (for use on the animal's skin as opposed to a product for the house or yard), which will kill the pest, making for easy removal. The best way to keep your Chow free from the ills of ticks is to check him every day.

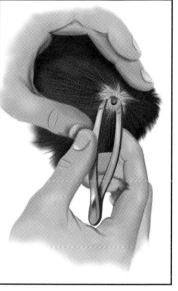

INTERNAL PARASITES

Roundworms These long, white worms are a common internal parasite, especially of puppies, although they occasionally infest adult dogs and people. The adult female roundworm can lay up to 200,000 eggs a day, which are passed in the dog's feces. Roundworms are transmitted through the feces of infected animals, so it's important you pick up your own dog's stools daily and prevent your dog from investigating other dogs' feces too closely.

Use tweezers to remove ticks from your dog.

If treated early, roundworms are not serious. A heavy infestation, however, can severely affect a dog's health. Puppies with roundworms appear thin, with a dull coat and potbelly. They will not thrive no matter what they eat. In people, roundworms can be more serious; therefore, early treatment, regular fecal checks and good sanitation are important.

Hookworms Hookworms live their adult lives in the dog's small intestines, where they attach to the intestinal wall and suck blood. When they detach and move to a new location, the old wound continues to bleed because of the anticoagulant the worm injects when it bites. Because of this, bloody diarrhea is usually the first sign of a problem.

Hookworm eggs, like roundworms, are passed through the feces. They are picked up either from the stools or, if conditions are right, from the soil. This is because the eggs can hatch in the soil, and when a host walks over infested soil, the worms attach themselves to the feet of their new hosts, burrowing into the skin and from there migrating to the intestinal tract, where the cycle starts all over again.

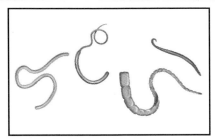

Common internal parasites (l-r): roundworm, whipworm, tapeworm and hookworm.

People, too, can pick up hookworms by walking barefoot in infected soil. In the Sunbelt states, children often pick up hookworm eggs when playing outside in the dirt or in a sandbox. Treatment, for both dogs and people, may have to be repeated.

Tapeworms   Tapeworms are also intestinal feeders, attaching to the intestinal wall to absorb nutrients. They grow by creating new segments. Usually the first sign of an infestation is the ricelike segments found in the stools or on the dog's coat near the rectum. Fleas are the intermediate hosts for tapeworms, and dogs get them when they chew a fleabite and swallow the flea. Therefore, a good flea control program is the best way to prevent a tapeworm infestation.

Whipworms   Adult whipworms live in the large intestine, where they feed on blood. The eggs are passed in the stool and can live in the soil for many years. If your dog eats the fresh spring grass, or buries her bone in the yard, she can pick up eggs from the infected soil. If you garden, you can pick up eggs under your fingernails, infecting yourself if you touch your face.

Heavy infestations cause diarrhea, often watery or bloody. The dog may appear thin and anemic, with poor coat. Severe bowel problems may result. Unfortunately, whipworm can be difficult to detect, as the worms do not continually shed eggs. Therefore a stool sample may be clear one day and show eggs the next.

Giardia Giardia is not a worm. It is a protozoan that infects animals through water. Giardia are common to wild animals in many areas, so your Chow Chow can pick it up from drinking from a water source where wild animals are living. That's why it's a good idea to bring water from home if you do any exploring of wild areas with your Chow. Diarrhea is one of the first symptoms of giardiasis, a giardial infection. If your dog has diarrhea and you and your dog have been out camping, make sure you tell your veterinarian.

Heartworms Pet owners hear a lot about heartworm these days. Heartworm is spread by infected mosquitoes (the intermediate host), which are common to many parts of the country. In most areas, dogs are put on heartworm preventative for most if not all of the year; this is because heartworm is so much easier to prevent than to cure.

You'll want to run your hands over your Chow Chow every day to check for cuts, parasites or anything strange on his skin.

Adult heartworms live in the upper heart and greater pulmonary arteries, where they severely damage the vessel walls. They are large worms and quickly clog the heart and pulmonary arteries. Poor circulation results, which in turn causes damage to other bodily functions; eventually, death from heart failure results.

Before starting a heartworm preventive treatment, your dog *must* be tested for the presence of heartworm and the results must be negative.

First Aid and Emergencies

The following are examples of problems that require
first aid. The advice is minimal and is not intended as
a substitute for veterinary care. Do what you can to
help your dog, then call your veterinarian.

TYPICAL FIRST-AID SITUATIONS

Your Chow Chow can't tell you when something's
wrong with him. But if you spend any time with
your dog, you'll be able to tell when he's not feeling
well. When you notice anything unusual in the way he's
acting, ask yourself these questions:

> What caused you to think there was a problem?
>
> What was your first clue there was something
> wrong?
>
> Is your Chow Chow eating normally?
>
> Does your Chow have a temperature? (Read on for
> instructions on taking your dog's temperature.)
>
> What do his stools look like?
>
> Is your Chow limping?
>
> When you do a hands-on exam, is he sore any-
> where? Can you feel a lump? Is anything red or
> swollen?

Write down anything you've noticed. When you call
your veterinarian, be prepared to give specific details
about your Chow Chow.

IN AN EMERGENCY

If something happens to your Chow Chow during non-
regular veterinary visiting hours, it's important to have
an emergency number to call. Ask your veterinarian
for this number on your first visit, and keep it by the
phone. You won't want to be scrambling for it when a
real emergency strikes. And you won't want to be strug-
gling with directions in the middle of the night if

you've never been to the emergency clinic before. It's a good idea to do a practice run to the emergency clinic during a non-emergency. You'll need all the calm you can muster in a real emergency, and knowing how long it will take to get to the clinic is important.

Fever Your vet will ask whether your dog has a fever. You can **take your dog's temperature** using a rectal thermometer (the kind used for people). A dog's normal temperature is between 101 and 102 degrees Fahrenheit. Shake the thermometer down and put some petroleum jelly on it. If possible, ask someone to help you by holding your Chow at his head so that he can't squirm around too much. Lift up your Chow's tail and insert the thermometer into the anus about one inch. Don't let go of it! Keep holding the thermometer and watch your clock. After three minutes, withdraw the thermometer, wipe it off and read the temperature.

Vomiting Your veterinarian will also ask whether your dog is vomiting. He or she will also ask what the vomit looked like. Is it vomit (digested food) or regurgitated food (which never makes it further than the esophagus and looks like slime-covered food)? Was there anything unusual in it, like garbage or glass or plant matter? Was it one instance or several?

Unusual Bowel Movements Similar questions will be asked about the dog's bowel movements. Did the dog have a bowel movement? If so, did it look normal? Was there

A FIRST-AID KIT
Keep a canine first-aid kit on hand for general care and emergencies. Check it periodically to make sure liquids haven't spilled or dried up, and replace medications and materials after they're used. Your kit should include:
Activated charcoal tablets
Adhesive tape (1 and 2 inches wide)
Antibacterial ointment (for skin and eyes)
Aspirin (buffered or enteric coated, *not* Ibuprofen)
Bandages: Gauze rolls (1 and 2 inches wide) and dressing pads
Cotton balls
Diarrhea medicine
Dosing syringe
Hydrogen peroxide (3%)
Petroleum jelly
Rectal thermometer
Rubber gloves
Rubbing alcohol
Scissors
Tourniquet
Towel
Tweezers

mucus or blood in the stool? Did the stool have a different or peculiar smell? Did you see any foreign objects in the stool?

Your veterinarian will still want to see your Chow Chow to be sure, but your answers to these questions will help a lot to establish an early diagnosis and to prepare your veterinarian for what to expect when you come in.

There are some problems you'll need to handle to some extent yourself before you bring your Chow to the veterinarian.

Animal Bites   If your Chow is bitten by another dog or other animal and he's in pain, you'll need to put a temporary muzzle on him. That way you can touch the area of the wound without getting bitten or snapped at. To make the muzzle, use a pair of panty hose or a long piece of gauze: Wrap it around the dog's muzzle, cross it under the jaw, and then pull it around the dog's head, tying it in the back.

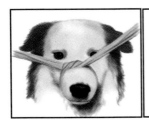

Use a scarf or old hose to make a temporary muzzle, as shown.

Trim the hair from around the wound and pour hydrogen peroxide liberally over it. A hand-held pressure bandage can help stop the bleeding. Stitches may be necessary if the bite is a rip or tear. Your veterinarian may also recommend putting the dog on antibiotics. Make sure the other animal was not rabid. If you can't be sure but you suspect it was, tell your veterinarian immediately.

Bee Stings   Many dogs are allergic to bee stings. You'll know if yours is, because the sting will start to swell immediately. Waste no time in getting your dog to the vet, who will give him an antihistamine or other treatment.

Bleeding Muzzle your dog if she is in pain. Place a gauze pad or a clean cloth over the wound, and apply pressure to stop the bleeding. If the wound will require stitches or if the bleeding doesn't stop, call your vet. If the wound is on a leg and continues to bleed, apply a tourniquet but make sure it is loosened every fifteen minutes. Get to your vet as soon as possible.

Choking If your Chow Chow is pawing at her mouth, gagging, coughing or drooling, she may have something caught in her mouth or throat. Open her jaws and shine a flashlight down her throat. If you can see the object, reach in and pull it out, using your fingers, tweezers or a pair of pliers. If you cannot see anything and your dog is still choking, hit her behind the neck between the shoulders to try and dislodge the object. If this fails, use an adapted Heimlich maneuver or abdominal thrust. For the Heimlich maneuver, with your dog standing, grasp either side of the rib cage and squeeze. Don't hurt her ribs, but try to make a sharp enough movement to cause the air in the lungs to force the object out. For the abdominal thrust, lay your dog on her side and, using your palms together, press in quick, sharp motions just behind the rib cage.

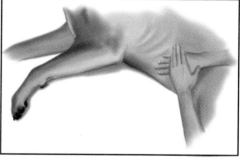

Applying abdominal thrusts can save a choking dog.

If your dog can breathe around the object, get to the vet as soon as possible. If your dog cannot breathe around the object, you don't have time to move her. Keep working on getting the object dislodged.

Diarrhea Diarrhea can be caused by many things, but it all comes out as loose, watery stools. (Severe diarrhea, which is accompanied by straining and blood in the stools, is called colitis.) Basically, diarrhea occurs when your dog eats something he shouldn't, like garbage, spoiled food, another animal's feces, plants, and so on. Once the offending matter has passed, the diarrhea goes away. You can help your dog feel better by feeding small meals of a bland diet such as boiled meat and plain rice, making sure there's plenty of water available (diarrhea is extremely dehydrating), and giving your dog an antidiarrheal medicine such as Loperamide. If the diarrhea persists or looks particularly bad, consult your veterinarian immediately.

Fractures   Because your Chow Chow will be in great pain if he has broken a bone, you should muzzle him immediately. Do not try to set the fracture, but try to immobilize the limb in a temporary splint by using a piece of wood and then wrapping it with gauze or soft cloth. If you can use a door or board as a backboard or stretcher so that the injured limb stays stable, use it. Transport the dog to the vet as soon as possible.

Make a temporary splint by wrapping the leg in firm casing, then bandaging it.

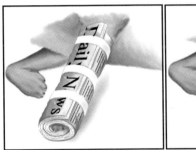 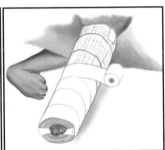

Broken Nails   A ripped or broken toenail can be very painful. If the dog is frantic, muzzle her to protect yourself. If a piece of the nail is hanging, trim it off; then run hydrogen peroxide over the nail. If the nail is bleeding, run it over a soft bar of soap; the soap will help the nail clot. If the quick is showing or if the nail has broken off under the skin, call your veterinarian; antibiotics might be needed to prevent an infection.

Overheating or Heatstroke   If your Chow is too warm and has difficulty breathing, starts panting rapidly, vomits or collapses, you need to act at once. These are all symptoms of heatstroke, which can be life-threatening. First, check your Chow's tongue. If his usually blue-black tongue shows lighter patches or pink blotches, your diagnosis is confirmed and your dog needs to be cooled *at once*. Immediately place your Chow in a tub of cool water (not freezing cold water) or, if a tub is not available, run water from a hose over your dog. Take his temperature and encourage him to drink some cool water. Call your veterinarian immediately.

Poisoning There is a host of products and plants that can be toxic to your Chow Chow. Antifreeze is one, and dogs are attracted to it because it tastes sweet. Household chemicals, insecticides, paints and various plants are all dangerous to inquiring mouths, which puppies certainly have!

Symptoms of poisoning include retching and vomiting, diarrhea, salivation, labored breathing, dilated pupils, weakness, collapse or convulsions. Sometimes one or more symptoms will appear, depending on the poison. If you suspect your dog has been in contact with a poison, timing is critical. Call your veterinarian right away. If your vet is not immediately available, call the National Animal Poison Control Center hotline (1-800-548-2423). The hotline and your vet can better treat your dog if you can tell them what was ingested and approximately how much. *Do not make your dog vomit unless instructed to do so.*

Some of the many household substances harmful to your dog.

Giving Your Chow Medicine

Some medicines are easy to administer; some are not. Some dogs will take pills or let you put ointment in their eyes easily; some will not. Ask your veterinarian for help, and follow these instructions.

To put eye ointment in the eye without poking the dog with the tube, stand behind your dog and cuddle his head up against your legs. With one hand, gently pull the lower eyelid away from the eye just slightly. At the same time, squeeze some of the ointment into the lower eyelid. When the dog closes his eye, the medication will be distributed over the eye.

To give a pill,
open the mouth
wide, then drop
it in the back of
the throat.

There are a couple of different ways to **give your dog a pill**. The easiest way is to keep a jar of baby food on hand. Dip the pill in it and your Chow should readily lick the pill (with baby food) right from your hand. For those who lick up the food and spit out the pill, you'll need to be more careful. Have your Chow

sit, and stand behind him, straddling his back. With the pill in one hand, pull your dog's head up and back gently so that his muzzle is pointing up. Open his mouth and very quickly drop the pill in at the back of his throat. Close his mouth and massage his throat until he swallows. Before you let him go, open his mouth and check to see whether the pill's gone. Follow up with a treat.

You can give **liquid medication** the same way, pouring it into your dog's mouth. Be careful that your Chow doesn't inhale the medication rather than swallow it.

An easier way is to measure the medicine into a chicken or turkey baster or a large eyedropper, put the tip of the baster into the dog's mouth from the side (between the molars) and, holding the dog's mouth shut, squeeze the medication in while you tilt his head backward slightly so that the medicine runs into instead of out of the mouth.

Applying **skin ointments** is usually very easy: Just part the hair so that you're

Squeeze eye oint-
ment into the
lower lid.

putting the ointment directly on the skin, and rub it in according to directions. Keeping your Chow from licking the ointment off can be more difficult, and licking often makes matters worse. If your dog has a bad skin condition or stitches that need to heal, your veterinarian will probably give you an Elizabethan collar for him. Named for the fashion styles of the reign of Queen Elizabeth I, this is a large plastic collar that extends at least to the tip of your dog's nose. The collar is ugly and clumsy, and most dogs absolutely hate it, but it's the only way the wound will have a chance to heal.

Remember, whenever your veterinarian prescribes a treatment or medication, don't be afraid to ask questions. Ask what the drug(s) is, what it does and how long your dog should take it. Ask whether there are any side effects you should watch for. Make sure you understand what your dog's problem is, what the course of treatment will do and what you should (or should not) expect. That done, make sure you follow through on the course of treatment. If your veterinarian said to give the medication for ten days, give it for ten days; don't stop at five days just because your dog looks better. Again, if you have any problems or reservations, call your vet.

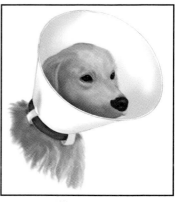

An Elizabethan collar keeps your dog from licking a fresh wound.

Medical Conditions to Which Chows Are Prone

Because of their size, skin type and other factors, Chow Chows are prone to entropion, hip dysplasia, luxating patellas, bloat, skin problems and obesity. Don't be unduly alarmed; so are many other breeds. With proper and conscientious care, you can use your awareness of these conditions to help spot their early warning signs (if they should occur at all) and thus help you get treatment for your Chow at the earliest possible stages.

Entropion   Entropion is a condition of the eyelids, in which the eyelid rolls inward. Entropion causes the eyelashes on the eyelid to irritate the surface of the eye. Most cases of entropion require surgical treatment, although in mild cases the dog may be fine with daily applications of eye ointment. In either case, dogs with entropion need regular eye care to keep the area clear.

Hip Dysplasia   This is a condition in which the structure of the hip joint undergoes changes. In normal hips, the head of the femur (thigh bone) fits into the acetabulum (cup of the hip). Dysplastic hips show a loosening or separation of the femur from the acetabulum. The condition can progress to the stage where a dog is unable to walk.

According to David Watkins, D.V.M., of the Animal Health Center in Sarasota, Florida, hip dysplasia is

common in Chow Chows. He advises owners to notify their veterinarians at the first sign of any lameness in their dogs, and to have their dogs' hips x-rayed at the age of six to nine months, when they come in to be spayed or neutered. Treatment depends on the severity of the dysplasia and ranges from relieving the pain with an anti-inflammatory to surgery.

An organization called the Orthopedic Foundation for Animals (OFA) reviews hip X rays and grades the hips. Dogs must be x-rayed at age twenty-four months or older. If the hips are normal,

Run your hands regularly over your dog to feel for any injuries.

the dog will receive an OFA number. That's why it's important, when looking for a Chow Chow puppy, to inquire about the puppy's parents' OFA ratings, or whether the hips have been checked at all. You can contact the OFA at 2300 E. Nifong Blvd., Columbia, MO 65201-3856.

Luxating Patella   The patella is the kneecap, and luxation is the medical term for dislocation, so a luxating patella is a dislocated kneecap. Owners can detect this condition in their dogs when the animal is moving and the knee sticks out to the side or seems to pop out. This is seen in puppies as young as four months. The treatment of choice is surgery to reconstruct the knee.

Bloat   This is a condition in which the dog's stomach becomes overinflated with gas. It usually strikes without warning and for reasons not altogether clear; fortunately, Chow Chows are not overly predisposed to it. To be on the safe side, Dr. Watkins advises owners not to exercise their dogs anytime soon after feeding dry food. Suspected causes are quick expansion of food inside the stomach, excessive drinking after eating, and gulping down food or water. If you notice your dog acting particularly lazy or drooling after eating, and if the stomach feels inflated and may be painful to the touch, call your veterinarian. Bloat can escalate into dilatation volvulus, which is a twisting of the gut that shuts off circulation—an extremely serious condition.

Your dog may crack a nail while out on a walk. Make sure you treat it as soon as possible to avoid infection.

Skin Problems   Because of their thick coats and fleshy skin, Chow Chows exhibit a number of skin problems, most notably flea allergy dermatitis, hot spots, atopies and staph infections. Flea allergy dermatitis is the skin's reaction to fleabites. Many dogs are allergic to the saliva a flea injects upon biting, and even one fleabite can cause them to itch themselves excessively. This leads to raw spots, often called hot spots, which do not heal easily because they involve a deeper layer of the skin. With a thick-coated breed like the Chow, it's especially important to be diligent about flea control. Daily grooming and inspection will alert an owner to the presence of fleas (see chapter 6).

An atopy is an allergic skin reaction. When it comes into contact with a substance to which it is allergic, the skin reacts by becoming inflamed, red and itchy. Allergies can develop by overexposure to the allergen (such as with flea allergy), or they can be genetic. Dogs can be allergic to types of food, cleaners, insect bites, smoke, pollens and any number of other things, just like people.

A staph infection is when the *staphylococcus* bacteria enters the skin through a cut or scrape. You'll notice red, pussy skin and small whiteheads, with irritation. Areas most affected are the groin, armpits and inner thighs. This is a common affliction of puppies under six months of age, and is treated with antibacterial soap and antibiotics.

Check your dog's teeth frequently and brush them regularly.

Dr. Watkins has treated a number of Chows for thyroid deficiency, which he has diagnosed after testing dogs with recurring skin problems. If your Chow's skin problems don't seem to get better with treatment, you should have the dog tested for thyroid deficiency.

Obesity The Chow Chow's heavy coat can sometimes mask a weight problem, because the dog's bulk may appear to be hair when in fact it's fat. The only solution is to feed less and exercise more. However, a problem with weight reduction even on a supervised diet can indicate a thyroid problem that should be checked by your veterinarian.

Aggression Though aggression is not a physical ailment, Dr. Watkins says this is a condition to which Chow Chows appear to be prone. As a Chow owner, you should be as mindful of this as you are of any of the other problems in this section. Dr. Watkins advises owners to establish leadership of their Chows early on (as discussed in depth in chapter 3). Behavior problems are the biggest killers of dogs, and when aware of their dogs' disposition to aggression, Chow owners are duty bound to socialize their puppies to prevent them from growing up into dangerous dogs.

As Your Chow Chow Ages

Chow Chows can, on the average, live twelve to fourteen years. To live that long in good health, however, your Chow Chow will need your help. Aging in dogs, as in people, involves some changes and problems. Your Chow's vision will dim, his hearing will fade and his joints will stiffen. Heart and kidney disease are common in older dogs. Reflexes will not be as sharp as they once were, and your dog may be more sensitive to heat and cold. Your dog may also get grouchy, showing less tolerance to younger dogs, children and other things that may not be part of his normal routine.

Arthritis Arthritis is common in old dogs. The joints get stiff, especially when it's chilly. Your Chow Chow may have trouble getting up in the morning. Make sure she has something soft and warm to sleep on not just at night, but all day. Talk to your veterinarian about treatment; there are pain relievers that can help.

Nutrition As your dog's activity level slows down, she will need to consume less calories and, as her body ages, she will need less protein. However, some old dogs have a problem digesting foods, too, and this may show up in poor stools and a dull coat. Several dog food manufacturers offer premium-quality foods for senior dogs, who digest these foods more easily.

Exercise Exercise is still important to your old Chow, who needs the stimulation of walking around and seeing and smelling the world. A leisurely walk around the neighborhood might be enough.

> ### WHEN TO CALL THE VET
>
> In any emergency situation, you should call your veterinarian immediately. You can make the difference in your dog's life by staying as calm as possible when you call and by giving the doctor or the assistant as much information as possible before you leave for the clinic. That way, the vet will be able to take immediate, specific action to remedy your dog's situation.
>
> Emergencies include acute abdominal pain, suspected poisoning, snakebite, burns, frostbite, shock, dehydration, abnormal vomiting or bleeding, and deep wounds. You are the best judge of your dog's health, as you live with and observe him every day. Don't hesitate to call your veterinarian if you suspect trouble.

When It's Time

There will come a time when you know your dog is suffering more than he needs to, and you will have to decide how to put him out of his pain. Only you can make the decision, but spare your companion the humiliation of incontinence, convulsions or the inability to stand up or move around. Your veterinarian can advise you on the condition of your dog, but don't let him or her make this decision for you.

When you know it's time, call your veterinarian. He or she can give your dog a tranquilizer, then an injection that is an overdose of anesthetic. Your already sleepy dog will quietly stop breathing. Be there with your dog. Let your arms hold your old friend and let your dog hear your voice saying how much you love him as he goes to sleep. There will be no fear, and the last thing your dog will remember is your love.

Your Chow Chow can live a long and healthy life with your help and attention.

GRIEVING

A well-loved dog is an emotional investment of unparalleled returns. Unfortunately, our dogs' lives are entirely too short and we must learn to cope with inevitably losing them. Grief is a natural reaction to the loss of a loved one, whether it is a pet, a spouse, friend or family member. Grief has no set pattern; its intensity and duration are different for each person and for each loss.

Sometimes the best outlet for grief is a good hard cry. For others, talking about their pet is good therapy. It's especially helpful to talk to people who've also lost an old dog and can relate to your loss. You may want to bury your old friend in a special spot where you can go to remember the wonderful times you shared together. You could also ask your veterinarian about having your dog cremated and keeping his or her ashes in a special urn in your home.

Your Happy, Healthy Pet

Your Dog's Name _____

Name on Your Dog's Pedigree (if your dog has one) _____

_____

Where Your Dog Came From _____

_____

Your Dog's Birthday _____

Your Dog's Veterinarian

    Name _____

    Address _____

    Phone Number _____

    Emergency Number _____

Your Dog's Health

    Vaccines

    type _____ date given _____

    type _____ date given _____

    type _____ date given _____

    type _____ date given _____

    Heartworm

    date tested _____ type used_____ start date _____

Your Dog's License Number _____

Groomer's Name and Number _____

Dogsitter/Walker's Name and Number _____

Awards Your Dog Has Won

    Award _____ date earned _____

    Award _____ date earned _____

part three

Enjoying

your

Dog

chapter 8

Basic
Training

by Ian Dunbar, Ph.D., MRCVS

Training is the jewel in the crown—the most important aspect of doggy husbandry. There is no more important variable influencing dog behavior and temperament than the dog's education: A well-trained, well-behaved and good-natured puppydog is always a joy to live with, but an untrained and uncivilized dog can be a perpetual nightmare. Moreover, deny the dog an education and it will not have the opportunity to fulfill its own canine potential; neither will it have the ability to communicate effectively with its human companions.

Luckily, modern psychological training methods are easy, efficient and effective and, above all, considerably dog-friendly and user-friendly. Doggy education is as simple as it is enjoyable. But before you can have a good time play-training with your new dog, you have to learn what to do and how to do it. There is no bigger variable influencing the success of dog training than the *owner's* experience and expertise. *Before you embark on the dog's education, you must first educate yourself.*

Basic Training for Owners

Ideally, basic owner training should begin well *before* you select your dog. Find out all you can about your chosen breed first, then master rudimentary training and handling skills. If you already have your puppy/dog, owner training is a dire emergency—the clock is running! Especially for puppies, the first few weeks at home are the most important and influential days in the dog's life. Indeed, the cause of most adolescent and adult problems may be traced back to the initial days the pup explores his new home. This is the time to establish the *status quo*—to teach the puppy/dog how you would like him to behave and so prevent otherwise quite predictable problems.

In addition to consulting breeders and breed books such as this one (which understandably have a positive breed bias), seek out as many pet owners with your breed you can find. Good points are obvious. What you want to find out are the breed-specific *problems*, so you can nip them in the bud. In particular, you should talk to owners with *adolescent* dogs and make a list of all anticipated problems. Most important, *test drive* at least half a dozen adolescent and adult dogs of your breed yourself. An eight-week-old puppy is deceptively easy to handle, but she will acquire adult size, speed and strength in just four months, so you should learn now what to prepare for.

Puppy and pet dog training classes offer a convenient venue to locate pet owners and observe dogs in action. For a list of suitable trainers in your area, contact the Association of Pet Dog Trainers (see Chapter 13). You may also begin your basic owner training by observing other owners in class. Watch as many classes and test drive as many dogs as possible. Select an upbeat, dog-friendly, people-friendly, fun-and-games, puppydog pet training class to learn the ropes. Also, watch training videos and read training books (see Chapter 12). You must find out what to do and how to do it *before* you have to do it.

Principles of Training

Most people think training comprises teaching the dog to do things such as sit, speak and roll over, but even a four-week-old pup knows how to do these things already. Instead, the first step in training involves teaching the dog human words for each dog behavior and activity and for each aspect of the dog's environment. That way you, the owner, can more easily participate in the dog's domestic education by directing him to perform specific actions appropriately, that is, at the right time, in the right place, and so on. Training opens communication channels, enabling an educated dog to at least understand the owner's requests.

In addition to teaching a dog *what* we want her to do, it is also necessary to teach her *why* she should do what we ask. Indeed, 95 percent of training revolves around motivating the dog *to want to do* what we want. Dogs often understand what their owners want; they just don't see the point of doing it—especially when the owner's repetitively boring and seemingly senseless instructions are totally at odds with much more pressing and exciting doggy distractions. It is not so much the dog who is being stubborn or dominant; rather, it is the owner who has failed to acknowledge the dog's needs and feelings and to approach training from the dog's point of view.

The Meaning of Instructions

The secret to successful training is learning how to use training lures to predict or prompt specific behaviors—to coax the dog to do what you want *when* you want. Any highly valued object (such as a treat or toy) may be used as a lure, which the dog will follow with his eyes and nose. Moving the lure in specific ways entices the dog to move his nose, head and entire body in specific ways. In fact, by learning the art of manipulating various lures, it is possible to teach the dog to assume virtually any body position and perform any action. Once you have control over the expression of the dog's behaviors and can elicit any body position or behavior at will, you can easily teach the dog to perform on request.

Tell your dog what you want him to do, use a lure to entice him to respond correctly, then profusely praise

Teach your dog words for each activity he needs to know, like down.

and maybe reward him once he performs the desired action. For example, verbally request "Fido, sit!" while you move a squeaky toy upwards and backwards over the dog's muzzle (lure-movement and hand signal), smile knowingly as he looks up (to follow the lure) and sits down (as a result of canine anatomical engineering), then praise him to distraction ("Gooood Fido!"). Squeak the toy, offer a training treat and give your dog and yourself a pat on the back.

Being able to elicit desired responses over and over enables the owner to reward the dog over and over. Consequently, the dog begins to think training is fun. For example, the more the dog is rewarded for sitting, the more she enjoys sitting. Eventually the dog comes

Enjoying Your
Dog

to realize that, whereas most sitting is appreciated, sitting immediately upon request usually prompts especially enthusiastic praise and a slew of high-level rewards. The dog begins to sit on cue much of the time, showing that she is starting to grasp the meaning of the owner's verbal request and hand signal.

Why Comply?

Most dogs enjoy initial lure/reward training and are only too happy to comply with their owners' wishes. Unfortunately, repetitive drilling without appreciative feedback tends to diminish the dog's enthusiasm until he eventually fails to see the point of complying anymore. Moreover, as the dog approaches adolescence he becomes more easily distracted as he develops other interests. Lengthy sessions with repetitive exercises tend to bore and demotivate both parties. If it's not fun, the owner doesn't do it and neither does the dog.

Integrate training into your dog's life: The greater number of training sessions each day and the *shorter* they are, the more willingly compliant your dog will become. Make sure to have a short (just a few seconds) training interlude before every enjoyable canine activity. For example, ask your dog to sit to greet people, to sit before you throw his Frisbee, and to sit for his supper. Really, sitting is no different from a canine "please." Also, include numerous short training interludes during every enjoyable canine pastime, for example, when playing with the dog or when he is running in the park. In this fashion, doggy distractions may be effectively converted into rewards for training. Just as all games have rules, fun becomes training . . . and training becomes fun.

Eventually, rewards actually become unnecessary to continue motivating your dog. If trained with consideration and kindness, performing the desired behaviors will become self-rewarding and, in a sense, your dog will motivate himself. Just as it is not necessary to reward a human companion during an enjoyable walk in the park, or following a game of tennis, it is hardly necessary to reward our best friend—the dog—for walking by our side or while playing fetch. Human company during enjoyable activities is reward enough for most dogs.

Even though your dog has become self-motivating, it's still good to praise and pet him a lot and offer rewards once in a while, especially for a good job well done. And if for no other reason, praising and rewarding others is good for the human heart.

To train your dog, you need gentle hands, a loving heart and a good attitude.

Punishment

Without a doubt, lure/reward training is by far the best way to teach: Entice your dog to do what you want and then reward him for doing so. Unfortunately, a human shortcoming is to take the good for granted and to moan and groan at the bad. Specifically, the dog's many good behaviors are ignored while the owner focuses on punishing the dog for making mistakes. In extreme cases, instruction is *limited* to punishing mistakes made by a trainee dog, child, employee or husband, even though it has been proven punishment training is notoriously inefficient and ineffective and is decidedly unfriendly and combative. It teaches the dog that training is a drag, almost as quickly as it teaches the dog to dislike his trainer. Why treat our best friends like our worst enemies?

Punishment training is also much more laborious and time consuming. Whereas it takes only a finite amount of time to teach a dog what to chew, for example, it takes much, much longer to punish the dog for each and every mistake. Remember, *there is only one right way!* So why not teach that right way from the outset?!

To make matters worse, punishment training causes severe lapses in the dog's reliability. Since it is obviously impossible to punish the dog each and every time she misbehaves, the dog quickly learns to distinguish between those times when she must comply (so as to avoid impending punishment) and those times when she need not comply, because punishment is impossible. Such times include when the dog is off leash and only six feet away, when the owner is otherwise engaged (talking to a friend, watching television, taking a shower, tending to the baby or chatting on the telephone), or when the dog is left at home alone.

Instances of misbehavior will be numerous when the owner is away, because even when the dog complied in the owner's looming presence, he did so unwillingly. The dog was forced to act against his will, rather than moulding his will to want to please. Hence, when the owner is absent, not only does the dog know he need not comply, he simply does not want to. Again, the trainee is not a stubborn vindictive beast, but rather the trainer has failed to teach.

Punishment training invariably creates unpredictable Jekyll and Hyde behavior.

Trainer's Tools

Many training books extol the virtues of a vast array of training paraphernalia and electronic and metallic gizmos, most of which are designed for canine restraint, correction and punishment, rather than for actual facilitation of doggy education. In reality, most effective training tools are not found in stores; they come from within ourselves. In addition to a willing dog, all you really need is a functional human brain, gentle hands, a loving heart and a good attitude.

In terms of equipment, all dogs do require a quality buckle collar to sport dog tags and to attach the leash (for safety and to comply with local leash laws). Hollow chewtoys (like Kongs or sterilized longbones) and a dog bed or collapsible crate are a must for housetraining. Three additional tools are required:

1. specific lures (training treats and toys) to predict and prompt specific desired behaviors;
2. rewards (praise, affection, training treats and toys) to reinforce for the dog what a lot of fun it all is; and
3. knowledge—how to convert the dog's favorite activities and games (potential distractions to training) into "life-rewards," which may be employed to facilitate training.

The most powerful of these is *knowledge*. Education is the key! Watch training classes, participate in training classes, watch videos, read books, enjoy playtraining with your dog, and then your dog will say "Please," and your dog will say "Thank you!"

Housetraining

If dogs were left to their own devices, certainly they would chew, dig and bark for entertainment and then no doubt highlight a few areas of their living space with sprinkles of urine, in much the same way we decorate by hanging pictures. Consequently, when we ask a dog to live with us, we must teach him *where* he may dig and perform his toilet duties, *what* he may chew and *when* he may bark. After all, when left at home alone for many hours, we cannot expect the dog to amuse himself by completing crosswords or watching the soaps on TV!

Also, it would be decidedly unfair to keep the house rules a secret from the dog, and then get angry and punish the poor critter for inevitably transgressing rules he did not even know existed. Remember, without adequate education and guidance, the dog will be forced to establish his own rules—doggy rules—that most probably will be at odds with the owner's view of domestic living.

Since most problems develop during the first few days the dog is at home, prospective dog owners must be certain they are quite clear about the principles of housetraining *before* they get a dog. Early misbehaviors quickly become established as the status quo—

becoming firmly entrenched as hard-to-break bad habits, which set the precedent for years to come. Make sure to teach your dog good habits right from the start. Good habits are just as hard to break as bad ones!

Ideally, when a new dog comes home, try to arrange for someone to be present for as much as possible during the first few days (for adult dogs) or weeks for puppies. With only a little forethought, it is surprisingly easy to find a puppy sitter, such as a retired person, who would be willing to eat from your refrigerator and watch your television while keeping an eye on the newcomer to encourage the dog to play with chewtoys and to ensure he goes outside on a regular basis.

POTTY TRAINING

To teach the dog where to relieve himself:

1. never let him make a single mistake;
2. let him know where you want him to go; and
3. handsomely reward him for doing so: "GOOOOOOOD DOG!!!" liver treat, liver treat, liver treat!

PREVENTING MISTAKES

A single mistake is a training disaster, since it heralds many more in future weeks. And each time the dog soils the house, this further reinforces the dog's unfortunate preference for an indoor, carpeted toilet. *Do not let an unhousetrained dog have full run of the house if you are away from home or cannot pay full attention.* Instead, confine the dog to an area where elimination is appropriate, such as an outdoor run or, better still, a small, comfortable indoor kennel with access to an outdoor run. When confined in this manner, most dogs will naturally housetrain themselves.

If that's not possible, confine the dog to an area, such as a utility room, kitchen, basement or garage, where elimination may not be desired in the long run but as an interim measure it is certainly preferable to doing it all around the house. Use newspaper to cover the floor of the dog's day room. The newspaper may be used to soak up the urine and to wrap up and dispose of the feces. Once your dog develops a preferred spot for eliminating, it is only necessary to cover that part of the floor with newspaper. The smaller papered area may then be moved (only a little each day) towards the door to the outside. Thus the dog will develop the tendency to go to the door when he needs to relieve himself.

Never confine an unhousetrained dog to a crate for long periods. Doing so would force the dog to soil the crate and ruin its usefulness as an aid for housetraining (see the following discussion).

TEACHING WHERE

In order to teach your dog where you would like her to do her business, you have to be there to direct the proceedings—an obvious, yet often neglected, fact of life. In order to be there to teach the dog *where* to go, you need to know *when* she needs to go. Indeed, the success of housetraining depends on the owner's ability to predict these times. Certainly, a regular feeding schedule will facilitate prediction somewhat, but there is nothing like "loading the deck" and influencing the timing of the outcome yourself!

Whenever you are at home, make sure the dog is under constant supervision and/or confined to a small

The first few weeks at home are the most important and influential in your dog's life.

area. If already well trained, simply instruct the dog to
lie down in his bed or basket. Alternatively, confine the
dog to a crate (doggy den) or tie-down (a short, 18-
inch lead that can be clipped to an eye hook in the
baseboard). Short-term close confinement strongly
inhibits urination and defecation, since the dog does
not want to soil his sleeping area. Thus, when you
release the puppydog each hour, he will definitely
need to urinate immediately and defecate every third
or fourth hour. Keep the dog confined to his doggy
den and take him to his intended toilet area each hour,
every hour, and on the hour.

When taking your dog outside, instruct him to sit quietly before opening the door—he will soon learn to sit
by the door when he needs to go out!

TEACHING WHY

Being able to predict when the dog needs to go
enables the owner to be on the spot to praise and
reward the dog. Each hour, hurry the dog to the
intended toilet area in the yard, issue the appropriate
instruction ("Go pee!" or "Go poop!"), then give the
dog three to four minutes to produce. Praise and offer
a couple of training treats when successful. The treats
are important because many people fail to praise their
dogs with feeling . . . and housetraining is hardly the
time for understatement. So either loosen up and
enthusiastically praise that dog: "Wuzzzer-wuzzer-
wuzzer, hooooser good wuffer den? Hoooo went pee for
Daddy?" Or say "Good dog!" as best you can and offer
the treats for effect.

Following elimination is an ideal time for a spot of
playtraining in the yard or house. Also, an empty dog
may be allowed greater freedom around the house for
the next half hour or so, just as long as you keep an eye
out to make sure he does not get into other kinds of
mischief. If you are preoccupied and cannot pay full
attention, confine the dog to his doggy den once more
to enjoy a peaceful snooze or to play with his many
chewtoys.

If your dog does not eliminate within the allotted time outside—no biggie! Back to his doggy den, and then try again after another hour.

As I own large dogs, I always feel more relaxed walking an empty dog, knowing that I will not need to finish our stroll weighted down with bags of feces! Beware of falling into the trap of walking the dog to get it to eliminate. The good ol' dog walk is such an enormous highlight in the dog's life that it represents the single biggest potential reward in domestic dogdom. However, when in a hurry, or during inclement weather, many owners abruptly terminate the walk the moment the dog has done its business. This, in effect, severely punishes the dog for doing the right thing, in the right place at the right time. Consequently, many dogs become strongly inhibited from eliminating outdoors because they know it will signal an abrupt end to an otherwise thoroughly enjoyable walk.

Instead, instruct the dog to relieve himself in the yard prior to going for a walk. If you follow the above instructions, most dogs soon learn to eliminate on cue. As soon as the dog eliminates, praise (and offer a treat or two)—"Good dog! Let's go walkies!" Use the walk as a reward for eliminating in the yard. If the dog does not go, put him back in his doggy den and think about a walk later on. You will find with a "No feces–no walk" policy, your dog will become one of the fastest defecators in the business.

If you do not have a back yard, instruct the dog to eliminate right outside your front door prior to the walk. Not only will this facilitate clean up and disposal of the feces in your own trash can but, also, the walk may again be used as a colossal reward.

Chewing and Barking

Short-term close confinement also teaches the dog that occasional quiet moments are a reality of domestic living. Your puppydog is extremely impressionable during his first few weeks at home. Regular confinement at this time soon exerts a calming influence over the dog's personality. Remember, once the dog is housetrained and calmer, there will be a whole lifetime ahead for the dog to enjoy full run of the house and garden. On the other hand, by letting the newcomer have unrestricted access to the entire household and allowing him to run willy-nilly, he will most certainly develop a bunch of behavior problems in short order, no doubt necessitating confinement later in life. It would not be fair to remedially restrain and confine a dog you have trained, through neglect, to run free.

When confining the dog, make sure he always has an impressive array of suitable chewtoys. Kongs and sterilized longbones (both readily available from pet stores) make the best chewtoys, since they are hollow and may be stuffed with treats to heighten the dog's interest. For example, by stuffing the little hole at the top of a Kong with a small piece of freeze-dried liver, the dog will not want to leave it alone.

Remember, treats do not have to be junk food and they certainly should not represent extra calories. Rather, treats should be part of each dog's regular daily diet: Some food may be served in the dog's bowl for breakfast and dinner, some food may be used as training treats, and some food may be used for stuffing chewtoys. I regularly stuff my dogs' many Kongs with different shaped biscuits and kibble.

Make sure your puppy has suitable chewtoys.

The kibble seems to fall out fairly easily, as do the oval-shaped biscuits, thus rewarding the dog instantaneously for checking out the chewtoys. The bone-shaped biscuits fall out after a while, rewarding the dog for worrying at the chewtoy. But the triangular biscuits never come out. They remain inside the Kong as lures, maintaining the dog's fascination with its chewtoy. To further focus the dog's interest, I always make sure to flavor the triangular biscuits by rubbing them with a little cheese or freeze-dried liver.

If stuffed chewtoys are reserved especially for times the dog is confined, the puppydog will soon learn to enjoy quiet moments in her doggy den and she will quickly develop a chewtoy habit—a good habit! This is a simple *passive training* process; all the owner has to do is set up the situation and the dog all but trains herself—easy and effective. Even when the dog is given run of the house, her first inclination will be to indulge her rewarding chewtoy habit rather than destroying less-attractive household articles, such as curtains, carpets, chairs and compact disks. Similarly, a chewtoy chewer will be less inclined to scratch and chew herself excessively. Also, if the dog busies herself as a recreational chewer, she will be less inclined to develop into a recreational barker or digger when left at home alone.

Stuff a number of chewtoys whenever the dog is left confined and remove the extra-special-tasting treats when you return. Your dog will now amuse himself with his chewtoys before falling asleep and then resume playing with his chewtoys when he expects you to return. Since most owner-absent misbehavior happens right after you leave and right before your expected return, your puppydog will now be conveniently preoccupied with his chewtoys at these times.

Come and Sit

Most puppies will happily approach virtually anyone, whether called or not; that is, until they collide with

To teach come, call your dog, open your arms as a welcoming signal, wave a toy or a treat and praise for every step in your direction.

adolescence and develop other more important doggy interests, such as sniffing a multiplicity of exquisite odors on the grass. Your mission, Mr. and/or Ms. Owner, is to teach and reward the pup for coming reliably, willingly and happily when called—and you have just three months to get it done. Unless adequately reinforced, your puppy's tendency to approach people will self-destruct by adolescence.

Call your dog ("Fido, come!"), open your arms (and maybe squat down) as a welcoming signal, waggle a treat or toy as a lure, and reward the puppydog when he comes running. Do not wait to praise the dog until he reaches you—he may come 95 percent of the way and then run off after some distraction. Instead, praise the dog's *first* step towards you and continue praising enthusiastically for *every* step he takes in your direction.

When the rapidly approaching puppy dog is three lengths away from impact, instruct him to sit ("Fido, sit!") and hold the lure in front of you in an outstretched hand to prevent him from hitting you midchest and knocking you flat on your back! As Fido decelerates to nose the lure, move the treat upwards and backwards just over his muzzle with an upwards motion of your extended arm (palm-upwards). As the dog looks up to follow the lure, he will sit down (if he jumps up, you are holding the lure too high). Praise the dog for sitting. Move backwards and call him again. Repeat this many times over, always praising when Fido comes and sits; on occasion, reward him.

For the first couple of trials, use a training treat both as a lure to entice the dog to come and sit and as a reward for doing so. Thereafter, try to use different items as lures and rewards. For example, lure the dog with a Kong or Frisbee but reward her with a food treat. Or lure the dog with a food treat but pat her and throw a tennis ball as a reward. After just a few repetitions, dispense with the lures and rewards; the dog will begin to respond willingly to your verbal requests and hand signals just for the prospect of praise from your heart and affection from your hands.

Instruct every family member, friend and visitor how to get the dog to come and sit. Invite people over for a series of pooch parties; do not keep the pup a secret— let other people enjoy this puppy, and let the pup enjoy other people. Puppydog parties are not only fun, they easily attract a lot of people to help *you* train *your* dog. Unless you teach your dog *how* to meet people, that is, to sit for greetings, no doubt the dog will resort to jumping up. Then you and the visitors will get annoyed, and the dog will be punished. This is not fair. *Send out those invitations for puppy parties and teach your dog to be mannerly and socially acceptable.*

Even though your dog quickly masters obedient recalls in the house, his reliability may falter when playing in the back yard or local park. Ironically, it is *the owner* who has unintentionally trained the dog *not* to respond in these instances. By allowing the dog to play and run around and otherwise have a good time, but then to call the dog to put him on leash to take him home, the dog quickly learns playing is fun but training is a drag. Thus, playing in the park becomes a severe distraction, which works against training. Bad news!

Instead, whether playing with the dog off leash or on leash, request him to come at frequent intervals— say, every minute or so. On most occasions, praise and pet the dog for a few seconds while he is sitting, then tell him to go play again. For especially fast recalls, offer a couple of training treats and take the time to praise and pet the dog enthusiastically before releasing him. The dog will learn that coming when called is not necessarily the end of the play session, and neither is it the end of the world; rather, it signals an enjoyable, quality time-out with the owner before resuming play once more. In fact, playing in the park now becomes a very effective life-reward, which works to facilitate training by reinforcing each obedient and timely recall. Good news!

Sit, Down, Stand and Rollover

Teaching the dog a variety of body positions is easy for owner and dog, impressive for spectators and extremely useful for all. Using lure-reward techniques, it is possible to train several positions at once to verbal commands or hand signals (which impress the socks off onlookers).

Sit and *down*—the two control commands—prevent or resolve nearly a hundred behavior problems. For example, if the dog happily and obediently sits or lies down when requested, he cannot jump on visitors, dash out the front door, run around and chase its tail, pester other dogs, harass cats or annoy family, friends or strangers. Additionally, "sit" or "down" are better emergency commands for off-leash control.

It is easier to teach and maintain a reliable sit than maintain a reliable recall. *Sit* is the purest and simplest of commands—either the dog is sitting or he is not. If there is any change of circumstances or potential danger in the park, for example, simply instruct the dog to sit. If he sits, you have a number of options: allow the dog to resume playing when he is safe; walk up and put the dog on leash, or call the dog. The dog will be much more likely to come when called if he has already acknowledged his compliance by sitting. If the dog does not sit in the park—train him to!

Stand and *rollover-stay* are the two positions for examining the dog. Your veterinarian will love you to distraction if you take a little time to teach the dog to stand still and roll over and play possum. Also, your vet bills will be smaller. The rollover-stay is an especially useful command and is really just a variation of the down-stay: whereas the dog lies prone in the traditional down, she lies supine in the rollover-stay.

As with teaching come and sit, the training techniques to teach the dog to assume all other body positions on cue are user-friendly and dog-friendly. Simply give the appropriate request, lure the dog into the desired body position using a training treat or toy and then *praise* (and maybe reward) the dog as soon as he complies. Try not to touch the dog to get him to respond. If you teach the dog by guiding him into position, the dog will quickly learn that rump-pressure means sit, for example, but as yet you still have no control over your dog if he is just six feet away. It will still be necessary to teach the dog to sit on request. So do not make training a time-consuming two-step process; instead, teach the dog to sit to a verbal request or hand signal from the outset. Once the dog sits willingly when requested, by all means use your hands to pet the dog when he does so.

To teach *down* when the dog is already sitting, say "Fido, down!," hold the lure in one hand (palm down) and lower that hand to the floor between the dog's forepaws. As the dog lowers his head to follow the lure, slowly move the lure away from the dog just a fraction (in front of his paws). The dog will lie down as he stretches his nose forward to follow the lure. Praise the dog when he does so. If the dog stands up, you pulled the lure away too far and too quickly.

When teaching the dog to lie down from the standing position, say "down" and lower the lure to the floor as before. Once the dog has lowered his forequarters and assumed a play bow, gently and slowly move the lure *towards* the dog between his forelegs. Praise the dog as soon as his rear end plops down.

After just a couple of trials it will be possible to alternate sits and downs and have the dog energetically perform doggy push-ups. Praise the dog a lot, and after half a dozen or so push-ups reward the dog with a training treat or toy. You will notice the more energetically you move your arm—upwards (palm up) to get the dog to sit, and downwards (palm down) to get the dog to lie down—the more energetically the dog responds to your requests. Now try training the dog in silence and you will notice he has also learned to respond to hand signals. Yeah! Not too shabby for the first session.

To teach *stand* from the sitting position, say "Fido, stand," slowly move the lure half a dog-length away from the dog's nose, keeping it at nose level, and praise the dog as he stands to follow the lure. As soon

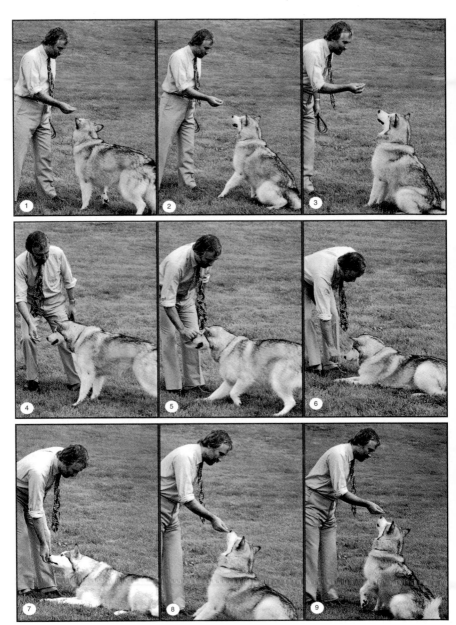

Using a food lure to teach sit, down and stand. 1) "Phoenix, Sit." 2) Hand palm upwards, move lure up and back over dog's muzzle. 3) "Good sit, Phoenix!" 4) "Phoenix, down." 5) Hand palm downwards, move lure down to lie between dog's forepaws. 6) "Phoenix, off. Good down, Phoenix!" 7) "Phoenix, sit!" 8) Palm upwards, move lure up and back, keeping it close to dog's muzzle. 9) "Good sit, Phoenix!"

10) "Phoenix, stand!" 11) Move lure away from dog at nose height, then lower it a tad. 12) "Phoenix, off! Good stand, Phoenix!" 13) "Phoenix, down!" 14) Hand palm downwards, move lure down to lie between dog's forepaws. 15) "Phoenix, off! Good down-stay, Phoenix!" 16) "Phoenix, stand!" 17) Move lure away from dog's muzzle up to nose height. 18) "Phoenix, off! Good stand-stay, Phoenix. Now we'll make the vet and groomer happy!"

as the dog stands, lower the lure to just beneath the dog's chin to entice him to look down; otherwise he will stand and then sit immediately. To prompt the dog to stand from the down position, move the lure half a dog-length upwards and away from the dog, holding the lure at standing nose height from the floor.

Teaching *rollover* is best started from the down position, with the dog lying on one side, or at least with both hind legs stretched out on the same side. Say "Fido, bang!" and move the lure backwards and alongside the dog's muzzle to its elbow (on the side of its outstretched hind legs). Once the dog looks to the side and backwards, very slowly move the lure upwards to the dog's shoulder and backbone. Tickling the dog in the goolies (groin area) often invokes a reflex-raising of the hind leg as an appeasement gesture, which facilitates the tendency to roll over. If you move the lure too quickly and the dog jumps into the standing position, have patience and start again. As soon as the dog rolls onto its back, keep the lure stationary and mesmerize the dog with a relaxing tummy rub.

To teach *rollover-stay* when the dog is standing or moving, say "Fido, bang!" and give the appropriate hand signal (with index finger pointed and thumb cocked in true Sam Spade fashion), then in one fluid movement lure him to first lie down and then rollover-stay as above.

Teaching the dog to *stay* in each of the above four positions becomes a piece of cake after first teaching the dog not to worry at the toy or treat training lure. This is best accomplished by hand feeding dinner kibble. Hold a piece of kibble firmly in your hand and softly instruct "Off!" Ignore any licking and slobbering *for however long the dog worries at the treat*, but say "Take it!" and offer the kibble *the instant* the dog breaks contact with his muzzle. Repeat this a few times, and then up the ante and insist the dog remove his muzzle for one whole second before offering the kibble. Then progressively refine your criteria and have the dog not touch your hand (or treat) for longer and longer periods on each trial, such as for two seconds, four seconds, then six, ten, fifteen, twenty, thirty seconds and so on. The dog soon learns: (1) worrying at the treat never gets results, whereas (2) noncontact is often rewarded after a variable time lapse.

Teaching *"Off!"* has many useful applications in its own right. Additionally, instructing the dog not to touch a training lure often produces spontaneous and magical stays. Request the dog to stand-stay, for example, and not to touch the lure. At first set your sights on a short two-second stay before rewarding the dog. (Remember, every long journey begins with a single step.) However, on subsequent trials, gradually and progressively increase the length of stay required to receive a reward. In no time at all your dog will stand calmly for a minute or so.

Relevancy Training

Once you have taught the dog what you expect her to do when requested to come, sit, lie down, stand, rollover and stay, the time is right to teach the dog *why* she should comply with your wishes. The secret is to have many (*many*) extremely short training interludes (two to five seconds each) at numerous (*numerous*) times during the course of the dog's day. Especially work with the dog immediately *before* the dog's good times and *during* the dog's good times. For example, ask your dog to sit and/or lie down each time before opening doors, serving meals, offering treats and tummy rubs; ask the dog to perform a few controlled doggy push-ups before letting her off-leash or throwing a tennis ball; and perhaps request the dog to sit-down-sit-stand-down-stand-rollover before inviting her to cuddle on the couch.

Similarly, request the dog to sit many times during play or on walks, and in no time at all the dog will be only too pleased to follow your instructions because he has learned that a compliant response heralds all sorts of goodies. Basically all you are trying to teach the dog is how to say please: "Please throw the tennis ball. Please may I snuggle on the couch."

Remember, whereas it is important to keep training interludes short, it is equally important to have many short sessions each and every day. The shortest (and most useful) session comprises asking the dog to sit and then go play during a play session. When trained this way, your dog will soon associate training with good times. In fact, the dog may be unable to distinguish between training and good times and, indeed, there should be no distinction. The warped concept that training involves forcing the dog to comply and/or dominating his will is totally at odds with the picture of a truly well-trained dog. In reality, enjoying a game of training with a dog is no different from enjoying a game of backgammon or tennis with a friend; and walking with a dog should be no different from strolling with buddies on the golf course.

Walk by Your Side

Many people attempt to teach a dog to heel by putting him on a leash and physically correcting the dog when he makes mistakes. There are a number of things seriously wrong with this approach, the first being that most people do not want precision heeling; rather, they simply want the dog to follow or walk by their side. Second, when physically restrained during "training," even though the dog may grudgingly mope by your side when "handcuffed" on leash, let's see what happens when he is off leash. History! The dog is in the next county because he never enjoyed walking with you on leash and you have no control over him off leash. So let's just teach the dog off leash from the outset to *want* to walk with us. Third, if the dog has not been trained to heel, it is a trifle hasty to think about punishing the poor dog for making mistakes and breaking heeling rules he didn't even know existed. This is simply not fair! Surely, if the dog had been adequately taught how to heel, he would seldom make mistakes and hence there would be no need to correct the dog. Remember, each mistake and each correction (punishment) advertise the trainer's inadequacy, not the dog's. The dog is not stubborn, he is not stupid and he is not bad. Even if he were, he would still require training, so let's train him properly.

Let's teach the dog to *enjoy* following us and to *want* to walk by our side offleash. Then it will be easier to teach high-precision off-leash heeling patterns if desired. After attaching the leash for safety on outdoor walks, but before going anywhere, it is necessary to teach the dog specifically not to pull. Now it will be much easier to teach on-leash walking and heeling because the dog already wants to walk with you, he is familiar with the desired walking and heeling positions and he knows not to pull.

FOLLOWING

Start by training your dog to follow you. Many puppies will follow if you simply walk away from them and maybe click your fingers or chuckle. Adult dogs may require additional enticement to stimulate them to follow, such as a training lure or, at the very least, a lively trainer. To teach the dog to follow: (1) keep walking and (2) walk away from the dog. If the dog attempts to lead or lag, change pace; slow down if the dog forges too far ahead, but speed up if he lags too far behind. Say "Steady!" or "Easy!" each time before you slow down and "Quickly!" or "Hustle!" each time before you speed up, and the dog will learn to change pace on cue. If the dog lags or leads too far, or if he wanders right or left, simply walk quickly in the opposite direction and maybe even run away from the dog and hide.

Practicing is a lot of fun; you can set up a course in your home, yard or park to do this. Indoors, entice the dog to follow upstairs, into a bedroom, into the bathroom, downstairs, around the living room couch, zigzagging between dining room chairs and into the kitchen for dinner. Outdoors, get the dog to follow around park benches, trees, shrubs and along walkways and lines in the grass. (For safety outdoors, it is advisable to attach a long line on the dog, but never exert corrective tension on the line.)

Remember, following has a lot to do with attitude—
your attitude! Most probably your dog will *not* want to
follow Mr. Grumpy Troll with the personality of wilted
lettuce. Lighten up—walk with a jaunty step, whistle a
happy tune, sing, skip and tell jokes to your dog and he
will be right there by your side.

BY YOUR SIDE

It is smart to train the dog to walk close on one side or
the other—either side will do, your choice. When walking, jogging or cycling, it is generally bad news to have
the dog suddenly cut in front of you. In fact, I train my
dogs to walk "By my side" and "Other side"—both very
useful instructions. It is possible to position the dog
fairly accurately by looking to the appropriate side and
clicking your fingers or slapping your thigh on that
side. A precise positioning may be attained by holding
a training lure, such as a chewtoy, tennis ball, or food
treat. Stop and stand still several times throughout the
walk, just as you would when window shopping or
meeting a friend. Use the lure to make sure the dog
slows down and stays close whenever you stop.

When teaching the dog to heel, we generally want
her to sit in heel position when we stop. Teach heel

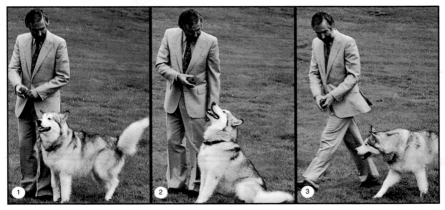

*Using a toy to teach sit-heel-sit sequences: 1) "Phoenix, heel!" Standing still, move lure up and back
over dog's muzzle.... 2) To position dog sitting in heel position on your left side. 3) "Phoenix, heel!"
wagging lure in left hand. Change lure to right hand in preparation for sit signal.*

position at the standstill and the dog will learn that the default heel position is sitting by your side (left or right—your choice, unless you wish to compete in obedience trials, in which case the dog must heel on the left).

Several times a day, stand up and call your dog to come and sit in heel position—"Fido, heel!" For example, instruct the dog to come to heel each time there are commercials on TV, or each time you turn a page of a novel, and the dog will get it in a single evening.

Practice straight-line heeling and turns separately. With the dog sitting at heel, teach him to turn in place. After each quarter-turn, half-turn or full turn in place, lure the dog to sit at heel. Now it's time for short straight-line heeling sequences, no more than a few steps at a time. Always think of heeling in terms of Sit-Heel-Sit sequences—start and end with the dog in position and do your best to keep him there when moving. Progressively increase the number of steps in each sequence. When the dog remains close for 20 yards of straight-line heeling, it is time to add a few turns and then sign up for a happy-heeling obedience class to get some advice from the experts.

4) Use hand signal only to lure dog to sit as you stop. Eventually, dog will sit automatically at heel whenever you stop. 5) "Good dog!"

NO PULLING ON LEASH

You can start teaching your dog not to pull on leash anywhere—in front of the television or outdoors—but regardless of location, you must not take a single step with tension in the leash. For a reason known only to dogs, even just a couple of paces of pulling on leash is intrinsically motivating and diabolically rewarding. Instead, attach the leash to the dog's collar, grasp the other end firmly with both hands held close to your chest, and stand still—do not budge an inch. Have somebody watch you with a stopwatch to time your progress, or else you will never believe this will work and so you will not even try the exercise, and your shoulder and the dog's neck will be traumatized for years to come.

Stand still and wait for the dog to stop pulling, and to sit and/or lie down. All dogs stop pulling and sit eventually. Most take only a couple of minutes; the all-time record is 22 ⅕ minutes. Time how long it takes. Gently praise the dog when he stops pulling, and as soon as he sits, enthusiastically praise the dog and take just one step forwards, then immediately stand still. This single step usually demonstrates the ballistic reinforcing nature of pulling on leash; most dogs explode to the end of the leash, so be prepared for the strain. Stand firm and wait for the dog to sit again. Repeat this half a dozen times and you will probably notice a progressive reduction in the force of the dog's one-step explosions and a radical reduction in the time it takes for the dog to sit each time.

As the dog learns "Sit we go" and "Pull we stop," she will begin to walk forward calmly with each single step and automatically sit when you stop. Now try two steps before you stop. Wooooooo! Scary! When the dog has mastered two steps at a time, try for three. After each success, progressively increase the number of steps in the sequence: try four steps and then six, eight, ten and twenty steps before stopping. Congratulations! You are now walking the dog on leash.

Whenever walking with the dog (off leash or on leash), make sure you stop periodically to practice a few position commands and stays before instructing the dog to "Walk on!" (Remember, you want the dog to be compliant everywhere, not just in the kitchen when his dinner is at hand.) For example, stopping every 25 yards to briefly train the dog amounts to over 200 training interludes within a single three-mile stroll. And each training session is in a different location. You will not believe the improvement within just the first mile of the first walk.

To put it another way, integrating training into a walk offers 200 separate opportunities to use the continuance of the walk as a reward to reinforce the dog's education. Moreover, some training interludes may comprise continuing education for the dog's walking skills: Alternate short periods of the dog walking calmly by your side with periods when the dog is allowed to sniff and investigate the environment. Now sniffing odors on the grass and meeting other dogs become rewards which reinforce the dog's calm and mannerly demeanor. Good Lord! Whatever next? Many enjoyable walks together of course. Happy trails!

THE IMPORTANCE OF TRICKS

Nothing will improve a dog's quality of life better than having a few tricks under its belt. Teaching any trick expands the dog's vocabulary, which facilitates communication and improves the owner's control. Also, specific tricks help prevent and resolve specific behavior problems. For example, by teaching the dog to fetch his toys, the dog learns carrying a toy makes the owner happy and, therefore, will be more likely to chew his toy than other inappropriate items.

More important, teaching tricks prompts owners to lighten up and train with a sunny disposition. Really, tricks should be no different from any other behaviors we put on cue. But they are. When teaching tricks, owners have a much sweeter attitude, which in turn motivates the dog and improves her willingness to comply. The dog feels tricks are a blast, but formal commands are a drag. In fact, tricks are so enjoyable, they may be used as rewards in training by asking the dog to come, sit and down-stay and then rollover for a tummy rub. Go on, try it: Crack a smile and even giggle when the dog promptly and willingly lies down and stays.

Most important, performing tricks prompts onlookers to smile and giggle. Many people are scared of dogs, especially large ones. And nothing can be more off-putting for a dog than to be constantly confronted by strangers who don't like him because of his size or the way he looks. Uneasy people put the dog on edge, causing him to back off and bark, only frightening people all the more. And so a vicious circle develops, with the people's fear fueling the dog's fear *and vice versa*. Instead, tie a pink ribbon to your dog's collar and practice all sorts of tricks on walks and in the park, and you will be pleasantly amazed how it changes people's attitudes toward your friendly dog. The dog's repertoire of tricks is limited only by the trainer's imagination. Below I have described three of my favorites:

SPEAK AND SHUSH

The training sequence involved in teaching a dog to bark on request is no different from that used when training any behavior on cue: request—lure—response—reward. As always, the secret of success lies in finding an effective lure. If the dog always barks at the doorbell, for example, say "Rover, speak!", have an accomplice ring the doorbell, then reward the dog for barking. After a few woofs, ask Rover to "Shush!", waggle a food treat under his nose (to entice him to sniff and thus to shush), praise him when quiet and eventually offer the treat as a reward. Alternate "Speak" and "Shush," progressively increasing the length of shush-time between each barking bout.

PLAYBOW

With the dog standing, say "Bow!" and lower the food lure (palm upwards) to rest between the dog's forepaws. Praise as the dog lowers her forequarters and sternum to the ground (as when teaching the down), but then lure the dog to stand and offer the treat. On successive trials, gradually increase the length of time the dog is required to remain in the playbow posture in order to gain a food reward. If the dog's rear end collapses into a down, say nothing and offer no reward; simply start over.

BE A BEAR

With the dog sitting backed into a corner to prevent him from toppling over backwards, say "Be a Bear!" With bent paw and palm down, raise a lure upwards and backwards along the top of the dog's muzzle. Praise the dog when he sits up on his haunches and offer the treat as a reward. To prevent the dog from standing on his hind legs, keep the lure closer to the dog's muzzle. On each trial, progressively increase the length of time the dog is required to sit up to receive a food reward. Since lure/reward training is so easy, teach the dog to stand and walk on his hind legs as well!

Teaching "Be a Bear"

chapter 9

Getting
Active
with your Dog

by Bardi McLennan

Once you and your dog have graduated from basic obedience training and are beginning to work together as a team, you can take part in the growing world of dog activities. There are so many fun things to do with your dog! Just remember, people and dogs don't always learn at the same pace, so don't be upset if you (or your dog) need more than two basic training courses before your team becomes operational. Even smart dogs don't go straight to college from kindergarten!

Just as there are events geared to certain types of dogs, so there are ones that are more appealing to certain types of people. In some activities, you give the commands and your dog does the work (upland game hunting is one example), while in others, such as agility, you'll both get a workout. You may want to aim for prestigious titles to add to your dog's name, or you may want nothing more than the sheer enjoyment of being around other people and their dogs. Passive or active, participation has its own rewards.

Consider your dog's physical capabilities when looking into any of the canine activities. It's easy to see that a Basset Hound is not built for the racetrack, nor would a Chihuahua be the breed of choice for pulling a sled. A loyal dog will attempt almost anything you ask him to do, so it is up to you to know your dog's limitations. A dog must be physically sound in order to compete at any level in athletic activities, and being mentally sound is a definite plus. Advanced age, however, may not be a deterrent. Many dogs still hunt and herd at ten or twelve years of age. It's entirely possible for dogs to be "fit at 50." Take your dog for a checkup, explain to your vet the type of activity you have in mind and be guided by his or her findings.

All dogs seem to love playing flyball.

You needn't be restricted to breed-specific sports if it's only fun you're after. Certain AKC activities are limited to designated breeds; however, as each new trial, test or sport has grown in popularity, so has the variety of breeds encouraged to participate at a fun level.

But don't shortchange your fun, or that of your dog, by thinking only of the basic function of her breed. Once a dog has learned how to learn, she can be taught to do just about anything as long as the size of the dog is right for the job and you both think it is fun and rewarding. In other words, you are a team.

To get involved in any of the activities detailed in this chapter, look for the names and addresses of the organizations that sponsor them in Chapter 13. You can also ask your breeder or a local dog trainer for contacts.

You can compete in obedience trials with a well trained dog.

Official American Kennel Club Activities

The following tests and trials are some of the events sanctioned by the AKC and sponsored by various dog clubs. Your dog's expertise will be rewarded with impressive titles. You can participate just for fun, or be competitive and go for those awards.

OBEDIENCE

Training classes begin with pups as young as three months of age in kindergarten puppy training, then advance to pre-novice (all exercises on lead) and go on to novice, which is where you'll start off-lead work. In obedience classes dogs learn to sit, stay, heel and come through a variety of exercises. Once you've got the basics down, you can enter obedience trials and work toward earning your dog's first degree, a C.D. (Companion Dog).

The next level is called "Open," in which jumps and retrieves perk up the dog's interest. Passing grades in competition at this level earn a C.D.X. (Companion Dog Excellent). Beyond that lies the goal of the most ambitious—Utility (U.D. and even U.D.X. or OTCh, an Obedience Champion).

AGILITY

All dogs can participate in the latest canine sport to have gained worldwide popularity for its fun and excitement, agility. It began in England as a canine version of horse show-jumping, but because dogs are more agile and able to perform on verbal commands, extra feats were added such as climbing, balancing and racing through tunnels or in and out of weave poles. Many of the obstacles (regulation or homemade) can be set up in your own backyard. If the agility bug bites, you could end up in international competition!

For starters, your dog should be obedience trained, even though, in the beginning, the lessons may all be taught on lead. Once the dog understands the commands (and you do, too), it's as easy as guiding the dog over a prescribed course, one obstacle at a time. In competition, the race is against the clock, so wear your running shoes! The dog starts with 200 points and the judge deducts for infractions and misadventures along the way.

All dogs seem to love agility and respond to it as if they were being turned loose in a playground paradise. Your dog's enthusiasm will be contagious; agility turns into great fun for dog and owner.

FIELD TRIALS AND HUNTING TESTS

There are field trials and hunting tests for the sporting breeds—retrievers, spaniels and pointing breeds, and for some hounds—Bassets, Beagles and Dachshunds. Field trials are competitive events that test a dog's ability to perform the functions for which she was bred. Hunting tests, which are open to retrievers,

---

TITLES AWARDED BY THE AKC

Conformation: Ch. (Champion)

Obedience: CD (Companion Dog); CDX (Companion Dog Excellent); UD (Utility Dog); UDX (Utility Dog Excellent); OTCh. (Obedience Trial Champion)

Field: JH (Junior Hunter); SH (Senior Hunter); MH (Master Hunter); AFCh. (Amateur Field Champion); FCh. (Field Champion)

Lure Coursing: JC (Junior Courser); SC (Senior Courser)

Herding: HT (Herding Tested); PT (Pre-Trial Tested); HS (Herding Started); HI (Herding Intermediate); HX (Herding Excellent); HCh. (Herding Champion)

Tracking: TD (Tracking Dog); TDX (Tracking Dog Excellent)

Agility: NAD (Novice Agility); OAD (Open Agility); ADX (Agility Excellent); MAX (Master Agility)

Earthdog Tests: JE (Junior Earthdog); SE (Senior Earthdog); ME (Master Earthdog)

Canine Good Citizen: CGC

Combination: DC (Dual Champion—Ch. and Fch.); TC (Triple Champion—Ch., Fch., and OTCh.)

---

spaniels and pointing breeds only, are noncompetitive
and are a means of judging the dog's ability as well as
that of the handler.

Hunting is a very large and complex part of canine
sports, and if you own one of the breeds that hunts, the
events are a great treat for your dog and you. He gets
to do what he was bred for, and you get to work with
him and watch him do it. You'll be proud of and
amazed at what your dog can do.

Fortunately, the AKC publishes a series of booklets on
these events, which outline the rules and regulations
and include a glossary of the sometimes complicated
terms. The AKC also publishes newsletters for field tri-
alers and hunting test enthusiasts. The United Kennel
Club (UKC) also has informative materials for the
hunter and his dog.

*Retrievers and
other sporting
breeds get to do
what they're
bred to in hunt-
ing tests.*

HERDING TESTS AND TRIALS

Herding, like hunting, dates
back to the first known uses man
made of dogs. The interest in
herding today is widespread,
and if you own a herding breed,
you can join in the activity.
Herding dogs are tested for
their natural skills to keep a
flock of ducks, sheep or cattle
together. If your dog shows
potential, you can start at the
testing level, where your dog can
earn a title for showing an inherent herding ability.
With training you can advance to the trial level, where
your dog should be capable of controlling even difficult livestock in diverse situations.

LURE COURSING

The AKC Tests and Trials for Lure Coursing are open
to traditional sighthounds—Greyhounds, Whippets,

Borzoi, Salukis, Afghan Hounds, Ibizan Hounds and Scottish Deerhounds—as well as to Basenjis and Rhodesian Ridgebacks. Hounds are judged on overall ability, follow, speed, agility and endurance. This is possibly the most exciting of the trials for spectators, because the speed and agility of the dogs is awesome to watch as they chase the lure (or "course") in heats of two or three dogs at a time.

TRACKING

Tracking is another activity in which almost any dog can compete because every dog that sniffs the ground when taken outdoors is, in fact, tracking. The hard part comes when the rules as to what, when and where the dog tracks are determined by a person, not the dog! Tracking tests cover a large area of fields, woods and roads. The tracks are laid hours before the dogs go to work on them, and include "tricks" like cross-tracks and sharp turns. If you're interested in search-and-rescue work, this is the place to start.

This tracking dog is hot on the trail.

EARTHDOG TESTS FOR SMALL TERRIERS AND DACHSHUNDS

These tests are open to Australian, Bedlington, Border, Cairn, Dandie Dinmont, Smooth and Wire Fox, Lakeland, Norfolk, Norwich, Scottish, Sealyham, Skye, Welsh and West Highland White Terriers as well as Dachshunds. The dogs need no prior training for this terrier sport. There is a qualifying test on the day of the event, so dog and handler learn the rules on the spot. These tests, or "digs," sometimes end with informal races in the late afternoon.

Here are some of the extracurricular obedience and racing activities that are not regulated by the AKC or UKC, but are generally run by clubs or a group of dog fanciers and are often open to all.

Canine Freestyle This activity is something new on the scene and is variously likened to dancing, dressage or ice skating. It is meant to show the athleticism of the dog, but also requires showmanship on the part of the dog's handler. If you and your dog like to ham it up for friends, you might want to look into freestyle.

Lure coursing lets sighthounds do what they do best—run!

Scent Hurdle Racing Scent hurdle racing is purely a fun activity sponsored by obedience clubs with members forming competing teams. The height of the hurdles is based on the size of the shortest dog on the team. On a signal, one team dog is released on each of two side-by-side courses and must clear every hurdle before picking up its own dumbbell from a platform and returning over the jumps to the handler. As each dog returns, the next on that team is sent. Of course, that is what the dogs are supposed to do. When the dogs improvise (going under or around the hurdles, stealing another dog's dumbbell, and so forth), it no doubt frustrates the handlers, but just adds to the fun for everyone else.

Flyball This type of racing is similar, but after negotiating the four hurdles, the dog comes to a flyball box, steps on a lever that releases a tennis ball into the air, catches the ball and returns over the hurdles to the starting point. This game also becomes extremely fun for spectators because the dogs sometimes cheat by catching a ball released by the dog in the next lane. Three titles can be earned—Flyball Dog (F.D.), Flyball Dog Excellent (F.D.X.) and Flyball Dog Champion (Fb.D.Ch.)—all awarded by the North American Flyball Association, Inc.

Dogsledding The name conjures up the Rocky Mountains or the frigid North, but you can find dogsled clubs in such unlikely spots as Maryland, North Carolina and Virginia! Dogsledding is primarily for the Nordic breeds such as the Alaskan Malamutes, Siberian Huskies and Samoyeds, but other breeds can try. There are some practical backyard applications to this sport, too. With parental supervision, almost any strong dog could pull a child's sled.

Coming over the A-frame on an agility course.

These are just some of the many recreational ways you can get to know and understand your multifaceted dog better and have fun doing it.

chapter 10

Your Dog
and your
Family

by Bardi McLennan

Adding a dog automatically increases your family by one, no matter whether you live alone in an apartment or are part of a mother, father and six kids household. The single-person family is fair game for numerous and varied canine misconceptions as to who is dog and who pays the bills, whereas a dog in a houseful of children will consider himself to be just one of the gang, littermates all. One dog and one child may give a dog reason to believe they are both kids or both dogs.

Either interpretation requires parental supervision and sometimes speedy intervention.

As soon as one paw goes through the door into your home, Rufus (or Rufina) has to make many adjustments to become a part of your family. Your job is to make him fit in as painlessly as possible. An older dog may have some frame of reference from past experience, but to a 10-week-old puppy, everything is brand new: people, furniture, stairs, when and where people eat, sleep or watch TV, his own place and everyone else's space, smells, sounds, outdoors—everything!

Puppies, and newly acquired dogs of any age, do not need what we think of as "freedom." If you leave a new dog or puppy loose in the house, you will almost certainly return to chaotic destruction and the dog will forever after equate your homecoming with a time of punishment to be dreaded. It is unfair to give your dog what amounts to "freedom to get into trouble." Instead, confine him to a crate for brief periods of your absence (up to

Lots of pets get along with each other just fine.

three or four hours) and, for the long haul, a workday for example, confine him to one untrashable area with his own toys, a bowl of water and a radio left on (low) in another room.

For the first few days, when not confined, put Rufus on a long leash tied to your wrist or waist. This umbilical cord method enables the dog to learn all about you from your body language and voice, and to learn by his own actions which things in the house are NO! and which ones are rewarded by "Good dog." Housetraining will be easier with the pup always by your side. Speaking of which, accidents do happen. That goal of "completely housetrained" takes up to a year, or the length of time it takes the pup to mature.

The All-Adult Family

Most dogs in an adults-only household today are likely to be latchkey pets, with no one home all day but the dog. When you return after a tough day on the job, the dog can and should be your relaxation therapy. But going home can instead be a daily frustration.

Separation anxiety is a very common problem for the dog in a working household. It may begin with whines and barks of loneliness, but it will soon escalate into a frenzied destruction derby. That is why it is so important to set aside the time to teach a dog to relax when left alone in his confined area and to understand that he can trust you to return.

Let the dog get used to your work schedule in easy stages. Confine him to one room and go in and out of that room over and over again. Be casual about it. No physical, voice or eye contact. When the pup no longer even notices your comings and goings, leave the house for varying lengths of time, returning to stay home for a few minutes and gradually increasing the time away. This training can take days, but the dog is learning that you haven't left him forever and that he can trust you.

Any time you leave the dog, but especially during this training period, be casual about your departure. No anxiety-building fond farewells. Just "Bye" and go! Remember the "Good dog" when you return to find everything more or less as you left it.

If things are a mess (or even a disaster) when you return, greet the dog, take him outside to eliminate, and then put him in his crate while you clean up. Rant and rave in the shower! *Do not* punish the dog. You were not there when it happened, and the rule is: Only punish as you catch the dog in the act of wrongdoing. Obviously, it makes sense to get your latchkey puppy when you'll have a week or two to spend on these training essentials.

Family weekend activities should include Rufus whenever possible. Depending on the pup's age, now is the time for a long walk in the park, playtime in the backyard, a hike in the woods. Socializing is as important as health care, good food and physical exercise, so visiting Aunt Emma or Uncle Harry and the next-door neighbor's dog or cat is essential to developing an outgoing, friendly temperament in your pet.

If you are a single adult, socializing Rufus at home and away will prevent him from becoming overly protective of you (or just overly attached) and will also prevent such behavioral problems as dominance or fear of strangers.

Babies

Whether already here or on the way, babies figure larger than life in the eyes of a dog. If the dog is there first, let him in on all your baby preparations in the house. When baby arrives, let Rufus sniff any item of clothing that has been on the baby before Junior comes home. Then let Mom greet the dog first before introducing the new family member. Hold the baby down for the dog to see and sniff, but make sure someone's holding the dog on lead in case of any sudden moves. Don't play keep-away or tease the dog with the baby, which only invites undesirable jumping up.

Dogs are perfect confidants.

The dog and the baby are "family," and for starters can be treated almost as equals. Things rapidly change, however, especially when baby takes to creeping around on all fours on the dog's turf or, better yet, has yummy pudding all over her face and hands! That's when a lot of things in the dog's and baby's lives become more separate than equal.

Toddlers make terrible dog owners, but if you can't avoid the combination, use patient discipline (that is, positive teaching rather than punishment), and use time-outs before you run out of patience.

A dog and a baby (or toddler, or an assertive young child) should never be left alone together. Take the dog with you or confine him. With a baby or youngsters in the house, you'll have plenty of use for that wonderful canine safety device called a crate!

Young Children

Any dog in a house with kids will behave pretty much as the kids do, good or bad. But even good dogs and good children can get into trouble when play becomes rowdy and active.

Teach children how to play nicely with a puppy.

Legs bobbing up and down, shrill voices screeching, a ball hurtling overhead, all add up to exuberant frustration for a dog who's just trying to be part of the gang. In a pack of puppies, any legs or toys being chased would be caught by a set of teeth, and all the pups involved would understand that is how the game is played. Kids do not understand this, nor do parents tolerate it. Bring Rufus indoors before you have reason to regret it. This is time-out, not a punishment.

You can explain the situation to the children and tell them they must play quieter games until the puppy learns not to grab them with his mouth. Unfortunately, you can't explain it that easily to the dog. With adult supervision, they will learn how to play together.

Young children love to tease. Sticking their faces or wiggling their hands or fingers in the dog's face is teasing. To another person it might be just annoying, but it is threatening to a dog. There's another difference: We can make the child stop by an explanation, but the only way a dog can stop it is with a warning growl and then with teeth. Teasing is the major cause of children being bitten by their pets. Treat it seriously.

Older Children

The best age for a child to get a first dog is between the ages of 8 and 12. That's when kids are able to accept some real responsibility for their pet. Even so, take the child's vow of "I will never *ever* forget to feed (brush, walk, etc.) the dog" for what it's worth: a child's good intention at that moment. Most kids today have extra lessons, soccer practice, Little League, ballet, and so forth piled on top of school schedules. There will be many times when Mom will have to come to the dog's rescue. "I walked the dog for you so you can set the table for me" is one way to get around a missed appointment without laying on blame or guilt.

Kids in this age group make excellent obedience trainers because they are into the teaching/learning process themselves and they lack the self-consciousness of adults. Attending a dog show is something the whole family can enjoy, and watching Junior Showmanship may catch the eye of the kids. Older children can begin to get involved in many of the recreational activities that were reviewed in the previous chapter. Some of the agility obstacles, for example, can be set up in the backyard as a family project (with an adult making sure all the equipment is safe and secure for the dog).

Older kids are also beginning to look to the future, and may envision themselves as veterinarians or trainers or show dog handlers or writers of the next Lassie best-seller. Dogs are perfect confidants for these dreams. They won't tell a soul.

Other Pets

Introduce all pets tactfully. In a dog/cat situation, hold the dog, not the cat. Let two dogs meet on neutral turf—a stroll in the park or a walk down the street—with both on loose leads to permit all the normal canine ways of saying hello, including routine sniffing, circling, more sniffing, and so on. Small creatures such as hamsters, chinchillas or mice must be kept safe from their natural predators (dogs and cats).

Festive Family Occasions

Parties are great for people, but not necessarily for
puppies. Until all the guests have arrived, put the dog
in his crate or in a room where he won't be disturbed.
A socialized dog can join the fun later as long as
he's not underfoot, annoying guests or into the hors
d'oeuvres.

There are a few dangers to consider, too. Doors opening and closing can allow a puppy to slip out unnoticed
in the confusion, and you'll be organizing a search
party instead of playing host or hostess. Party food and
buffet service are not for dogs. Let Rufus party in his
crate with a nice big dog biscuit.

At Christmas time, not only are tree decorations dangerous and breakable (and perhaps family heirlooms),
but extreme caution should be taken with the lights,
cords and outlets for the tree lights and any other fes-
tive lighting. Occasionally a dog lifts a leg, ignoring the
fact that the tree is indoors. To avoid this, use a canine
repellent, made for gardens, on the tree. Or keep him
out of the tree room unless supervised. And whatever
you do, *don't* invite trouble by hanging his toys on the
tree!

Car Travel

Before you plan a vacation by car or RV with Rufus, be
sure he enjoys car travel. Nothing spoils a holiday
quicker than a carsick dog! Work within the dog's com-
fort level. Get in the car with the dog in his crate or
attached to a canine car safety belt and just sit there
until he relaxes. That's all. Next time, get in the car,
turn on the engine and go nowhere. Just sit. When that
is okay, turn on the engine and go around the block.
Now you can go for a ride and include a stop where
you get out, leaving the dog for a minute or two.

On a warm day, always park in the shade and leave windows open several inches. And return quickly. It only
takes 10 minutes for a car to become an overheated
steel death trap.

Motel or Pet Motel?

Not all motels or hotels accept pets, but you have a much better choice today than even a few years ago. To find a dog-friendly lodging, look at *On the Road Again With Man's Best Friend*, a series of directories that detail bed and breakfasts, inns, family resorts and other hotels/motels. Some places require a refundable deposit to cover any damage incurred by the dog. More B&Bs accept pets now, but some restrict the size.

If taking Rufus with you is not feasible, check out boarding kennels in your area. Your veterinarian may offer this service, or recommend a kennel or two he or she is familiar with. Go see the facilities for yourself, ask about exercise, diet, housing, and so on. Or, if you'd rather have Rufus stay home, look into bonded petsitters, many of whom will also bring in the mail and water your plants.

chapter 11

Your Dog
and your
Community

by Bardi McLennan

Step outside your home with your dog and you are no longer just family, you are both part of your community. This is when the phrase "responsible pet ownership" takes on serious implications. For starters, it means you pick up after your dog—not just occasionally, but every time your dog eliminates away from home. That means you have joined the Plastic Baggy Brigade! You always have plastic sandwich bags in your pocket and several in the car. It means you teach your kids how to use them, too. If you think this is "yucky," just imagine what

the person (a non-doggy person) who inadvertently steps in the mess thinks!

Your responsibility extends to your neighbors: To their ears (no annoying barking); to their property (their garbage, their lawn, their flower beds, their cat—especially their cat); to their kids (on bikes, at play); to their kids' toys and sports equipment.

There are numerous dog-related laws, ranging from simple dog licensing and leash laws to those holding you liable for any physical injury or property damage done by your dog. These laws are in place to protect everyone in the community, including you and your dog. There are town ordinances and state laws which are by no means the same in all towns or all states. Ignorance of the law won't get you off the hook. The time to find out what the laws are where you live is now.

Be sure your dog's license is current. This is not just a good local ordinance, it can make the difference between finding your lost dog or not. Many states now require proof of rabies vaccination and that the dog has been spayed or neutered before issuing a license. At the same time, keep up the dog's annual immunizations.

Dressing your dog up makes him appealing to strangers.

Never let your dog run loose in the neighborhood. This will not only keep you on the right side of the leash law, it's the outdoor version of the rule about not giving your dog "freedom to get into trouble."

Good Canine Citizen

Sometimes it's hard for a dog's owner to assess whether or not the dog is sufficiently socialized to be accepted by the community at large. Does Rufus or Rufina display good, controlled behavior in public? The AKC's Canine Good Citizen program is available through many dog organizations. If your dog passes the test, the title "CGC" is earned.

The overall purpose is to turn your dog into a good neighbor and to teach you about your responsibility to your community as a dog owner. Here are the ten things your dog must do willingly:

1. Accept a stranger stopping to chat with you.
2. Sit and be petted by a stranger.
3. Allow a stranger to handle him or her as a groomer or veterinarian would.
4. Walk nicely on a loose lead.
5. Walk calmly through a crowd.
6. Sit and down on command, then stay in a sit or down position while you walk away.
7. Come when called.
8. Casually greet another dog.
9. React confidently to distractions.
10. Accept being left alone with someone other than you and not become overly agitated or nervous.

Schools and Dogs

Schools are getting involved with pet ownership on an educational level. It has been proven that children who are kind to animals are humane in their attitude toward other people as adults.

A dog is a child's best friend, and so children are often primary pet owners, if not the primary caregivers. Unfortunately, they are also the ones most often bitten by dogs. This occurs due to a lack of understanding that pets, no matter how sweet, cuddly and loving, are still animals. Schools, along with parents, dog clubs, dog fanciers and the AKC, are working to change all that with video programs for children not only in grade school, but in the nursery school and pre-kindergarten age group. Teaching youngsters how to be responsible dog owners is important community work. When your dog has a CGC, volunteer to take part in an educational classroom event put on by your dog club.

Boy Scout Merit Badge

A Merit Badge for Dog Care can be earned by any Boy Scout ages 11 to 18. The requirements are not easy, but amount to a complete course in responsible dog care and general ownership. Here are just a few of the things a Scout must do to earn that badge:

Point out ten parts of the dog using the correct names.

Give a report (signed by parent or guardian) on your care of the dog (feeding, food used, housing, exercising, grooming and bathing), plus what has been done to keep the dog healthy.

Explain the right way to obedience train a dog, and demonstrate three comments.

Several of the requirements have to do with health care, including first aid, handling a hurt dog, and the dangers of home treatment for a serious ailment.

The final requirement is to know the local laws and ordinances involving dogs.

There are similar programs for Girl Scouts and 4-H members.

Local Clubs

Local dog clubs are no longer in existence just to put on a yearly dog show. Today, they are apt to be the hub of the community's involvement with pets. Dog clubs conduct educational forums with big-name speakers, stage demonstrations of canine talent in a busy mall and take dogs of various breeds to schools for classroom discussion.

The quickest way to feel accepted as a member in a club is to volunteer your services! Offer to help with something—anything—and watch your popularity (and your interest) grow.

Therapy Dogs

Once your dog has earned that essential CGC and reliably demonstrates a steady, calm temperament, you could look into what therapy dogs are doing in your area.

Therapy dogs go with their owners to visit patients at hospitals or nursing homes, generally remaining on leash but able to coax a pat from a stiffened hand, a smile from a blank face, a few words from sealed lips or a hug from someone in need of love.

Your dog can make a difference in lots of lives.

Nursing homes cover a wide range of patient care. Some specialize in care of the elderly, some in the treatment of specific illnesses, some in physical therapy. Children's facilities also welcome visits from trained therapy dogs for boosting morale in their pediatric patients. Hospice care for the terminally ill and the at-home care of AIDS patients are other areas where this canine visiting is desperately needed. Therapy dog training comes first.

There is a lot more involved than just taking your nice friendly pooch to someone's bedside. Doing therapy dog work involves your own emotional stability as well as that of your dog. But once you have met all the requirements for this work, making the rounds once a week or once a month with your therapy dog is possibly the most rewarding of all community activities.

Disaster Aid

This community service is definitely not for everyone, partly because it is time-consuming. The initial training is rigorous, and there can be no let-up in the continuing workouts, because members are on call 24 hours a day to go wherever they are needed at a moment's notice. But if you think you would like to be able to assist in a disaster, look into search-and-rescue work. The network of search-and-rescue volunteers is worldwide, and all members of the American Rescue Dog Association (ARDA) who are qualified to do this work are volunteers who train and maintain their own dogs.

Physical Aid

Most people are familiar with Seeing Eye dogs, which serve as blind people's eyes, but not with all the other work that dogs are trained to do to assist the disabled. Dogs are also specially trained to pull wheelchairs, carry school books, pick up dropped objects, open and close doors. Some also are ears for the deaf. All these assistance-trained dogs, by the way, are allowed anywhere "No Pet" signs exist (as are therapy dogs when properly identified). Getting started in any of this fascinating work requires a background in dog training and canine behavior, but there are also volunteer jobs ranging from answering the phone to cleaning out kennels to providing a foster home for a puppy. You have only to ask.

Making the rounds with your therapy dog can be very rewarding.

part four

Beyond the Basics

chapter 12

Recommended Reading

Books

ABOUT HEALTH CARE

Ackerman, Lowell. *Guide to Skin and Haircoat Problems in Dogs*. Loveland, Colo.: Alpine Publications, 1994.

Alderton, David. *The Dog Care Manual*. Hauppauge, N.Y.: Barron's Educational Series, Inc., 1986.

American Kennel Club. *American Kennel Club Dog Care and Training*. New York: Howell Book House, 1991.

Bamberger, Michelle, DVM. *Help! The Quick Guide to First Aid for Your Dog*. New York: Howell Book House, 1995.

Carlson, Delbert, DVM, and James Giffin, MD. *Dog Owner's Home Veterinary Handbook*. New York: Howell Book House, 1992.

DeBitetto, James, DVM, and Sarah Hodgson. *You & Your Puppy*. New York: Howell Book House, 1995.

Humphries, Jim, DVM. *Dr. Jim's Animal Clinic for Dogs*. New York: Howell Book House, 1994.

McGinnis, Terri. *The Well Dog Book*. New York: Random House, 1991.

Pitcairn, Richard and Susan. *Natural Health for Dogs*. Emmaus, Pa.: Rodale Press, 1982.

ABOUT DOG SHOWS

Hall, Lynn. *Dog Showing for Beginners*. New York: Howell Book House, 1994.

Nichols, Virginia Tuck. *How to Show Your Own Dog*. Neptune, N. J.: TFH, 1970.

Vanacore, Connie. *Dog Showing, An Owner's Guide*. New York: Howell Book House, 1990.

Beyond the
Basics

ABOUT TRAINING

Ammen, Amy. *Training in No Time.* New York: Howell Book House, 1995.

Baer, Ted. *Communicating With Your Dog.* Hauppauge, N.Y.: Barron's Educational Series, Inc., 1989.

Benjamin, Carol Lea. *Dog Problems.* New York: Howell Book House, 1989.

Benjamin, Carol Lea. *Dog Training for Kids.* New York: Howell Book House, 1988.

Benjamin, Carol Lea. *Mother Knows Best.* New York: Howell Book House, 1985.

Benjamin, Carol Lea. *Surviving Your Dog's Adolescence.* New York: Howell Book House, 1993.

Bohnenkamp, Gwen. *Manners for the Modern Dog.* San Francisco: Perfect Paws, 1990.

Dibra, Bashkim. *Dog Training by Bash.* New York: Dell, 1992.

Dunbar, Ian, PhD, MRCVS. *Dr. Dunbar's Good Little Dog Book,* James & Kenneth Publishers, 2140 Shattuck Ave. #2406, Berkeley, Calif. 94704. (510) 658–8588. Order from the publisher.

Dunbar, Ian, PhD, MRCVS. *How to Teach a New Dog Old Tricks,* James & Kenneth Publishers. Order from the publisher; address above.

Dunbar, Ian, PhD, MRCVS, and Gwen Bohnenkamp. Booklets on *Preventing Aggression; Housetraining; Chewing; Digging; Barking; Socialization; Fearfulness; and Fighting,* James & Kenneth Publishers. Order from the publisher; address above.

Evans, Job Michael. *People, Pooches and Problems.* New York: Howell Book House, 1991.

Kilcommons, Brian and Sarah Wilson. *Good Owners, Great Dogs.* New York: Warner Books, 1992.

McMains, Joel M. *Dog Logic—Companion Obedience.* New York: Howell Book House, 1992.

Rutherford, Clarice and David H. Neil, MRCVS. *How to Raise a Puppy You Can Live With.* Loveland, Colo.: Alpine Publications, 1982.

Volhard, Jack and Melissa Bartlett. *What All Good Dogs Should Know: The Sensible Way to Train.* New York: Howell Book House, 1991.

ABOUT BREEDING

Harris, Beth J. Finder. *Breeding a Litter, The Complete Book of Prenatal and Postnatal Care.* New York: Howell Book House, 1983.

Holst, Phyllis, DVM. *Canine Reproduction.* Loveland, Colo.: Alpine Publications, 1985.

Walkowicz, Chris and Bonnie Wilcox, DVM. *Successful Dog Breeding, The Complete Handbook of Canine Midwifery.* New York: Howell Book House, 1994.

ABOUT ACTIVITIES

American Rescue Dog Association. *Search and Rescue Dogs.* New York: Howell Book House, 1991.

Barwig, Susan and Stewart Hilliard. *Schutzhund.* New York: Howell Book House, 1991.

Beaman, Arthur S. *Lure Coursing.* New York: Howell Book House, 1994.

Daniels, Julie. *Enjoying Dog Agility—From Backyard to Competition.* New York: Doral Publishing, 1990.

Davis, Kathy Diamond. *Therapy Dogs.* New York: Howell Book House, 1992.

Gallup, Davis Anne. *Running With Man's Best Friend.* Loveland, Colo.: Alpine Publications, 1986.

Habgood, Dawn and Robert. *On the Road Again With Man's Best Friend.* New England, Mid-Atlantic, West Coast and Southeast editions. Selective guides to area bed and breakfasts, inns, hotels and resorts that welcome guests and their dogs. New York: Howell Book House, 1995.

Holland, Vergil S. *Herding Dogs.* New York: Howell Book House, 1994

LaBelle, Charlene G. *Backpacking With Your Dog.* Loveland, Colo.: Alpine Publications, 1993.

Simmons-Moake, Jane. *Agility Training, The Fun Sport for All Dogs.* New York: Howell Book House, 1991.

Spencer, James B. *Hup! Training Flushing Spaniels the American Way.* New York: Howell Book House, 1992.

Spencer, James B. *Point! Training the All-Seasons Birddog.* New York: Howell Book House, 1995.

Tarrant, Bill. *Training the Hunting Retriever.* New York: Howell Book House, 1991.

Volhard, Jack and Wendy. *The Canine Good Citizen.* New York: Howell Book House, 1994.

General Titles

Haggerty, Captain Arthur J. *How to Get Your Pet Into Show Business.* New York: Howell Book House, 1994.

McLennan, Bardi. *Dogs and Kids, Parenting Tips.* New York: Howell Book House, 1993.

Moran, Patti J. *Pet Sitting for Profit, A Complete Manual for Professional Success.* New York: Howell Book House, 1992.

Scalisi, Danny and Libby Moses. *When Rover Just Won't Do, Over 2,000 Suggestions for Naming Your Dog.* New York: Howell Book House, 1993.

Sife, Wallace, PhD. *The Loss of a Pet.* New York: Howell Book House, 1993.

Wrede, Barbara J. *Civilizing Your Puppy.* Hauppauge, N.Y.: Barron's Educational Series, 1992.

Magazines

The AKC GAZETTE, The Official Journal for the Sport of Purebred Dogs. American Kennel Club, 51 Madison Ave., New York, NY.

Bloodlines Journal. United Kennel Club, 100 E. Kilgore Rd., Kalamazoo, MI.

Dog Fancy. Fancy Publications, 3 Burroughs, Irvine, CA 92718

Dog World. Maclean Hunter Publishing Corp., 29 N. Wacker Dr., Chicago, IL 60606.

Videos

"SIRIUS Puppy Training," by Ian Dunbar, PhD, MRCVS. James & Kenneth Publishers, 2140 Shattuck Ave. #2406, Berkeley, CA 94704. Order from the publisher.

"Training the Companion Dog," from Dr. Dunbar's British TV Series, James & Kenneth Publishers. (See address above).

The American Kennel Club produces videos on every breed of dog, as well as on hunting tests, field trials and other areas of interest to purebred dog owners. For more information, write to AKC/Video Fulfillment, 5580 Centerview Dr., Suite 200, Raleigh, NC 27606.

chapter 13

Resources

Breed Clubs

Every breed recognized by the American Kennel Club has a national (parent) club. National clubs are a great source of information on your breed. You can get the name of the secretary of the club by contacting:

The American Kennel Club
51 Madison Avenue
New York, NY 10010
(212) 696-8200

There are also numerous all-breed, individual breed, obedience, hunting and other special-interest dog clubs across the country. The American Kennel Club can provide you with a geographical list of clubs to find ones in your area. Contact them at the above address.

Registry Organizations

Registry organizations register purebred dogs. The American Kennel Club is the oldest and largest in this country, and currently recognizes over 130 breeds. The United Kennel Club registers some breeds the AKC doesn't (including the American Pit Bull Terrier and the Miniature Fox Terrier) as well as many of the same breeds. The others included here are for your reference; the AKC can provide you with a list of foreign registries.

American Kennel Club
51 Madison Avenue
New York, NY 10010

United Kennel Club (UKC)
100 E. Kilgore Road
Kalamazoo, MI 49001-5598

American Dog Breeders Assn.
P.O. Box 1771
Salt Lake City, UT 84110
(Registers American Pit Bull Terriers)

Canadian Kennel Club
89 Skyway Avenue
Etobicoke, Ontario
Canada M9W 6R4

National Stock Dog Registry
P.O. Box 402
Butler, IN 46721
(Registers working stock dogs)

Orthopedic Foundation for Animals (OFA)
2300 E. Nifong Blvd.
Columbia, MO 65201-3856
(Hip registry)

Activity Clubs

Write to these organizations for information on the activities they sponsor.

American Kennel Club
51 Madison Avenue
New York, NY 10010
(Conformation Shows, Obedience Trials, Field
Trials and Hunting Tests, Agility, Canine Good

Citizen, Lure Coursing, Herding, Tracking,
Earthdog Tests, Coonhunting.)

United Kennel Club
100 E. Kilgore Road
Kalamazoo, MI 49001-5598
(Conformation Shows, Obedience Trials, Agility,
Hunting for Various Breeds, Terrier Trials and
more.)

North American Flyball Assn.
1342 Jeff St.
Ypsilanti, MI 48198

International Sled Dog Racing Assn.
P.O. Box 446
Norman, ID 83848-0446

North American Working Dog Assn., Inc.
Southeast Kreisgruppe
P.O. Box 833
Brunswick, GA 31521

Trainers

Association of Pet Dog Trainers
P.O. Box 3734
Salinas, CA 93912
(408) 663-9257

American Dog Trainers' Network
161 West 4th St.
New York, NY 10014
(212) 727-7257

**National Association of Dog Obedience
Instructors**
2286 East Steel Rd.
St. Johns, MI 48879

Associations

American Dog Owners Assn.
1654 Columbia Tpk.
Castleton, NY 12033
(Combats anti-dog legislation)

Delta Society
P.O. Box 1080
Renton, WA 98057-1080
(Promotes the human/animal bond through
pet-assisted therapy and other programs)

Dog Writers Assn. of America (DWAA)
Sally Cooper, Secy.
222 Woodchuck Ln.
Harwinton, CT 06791

National Assn. for Search and Rescue (NASAR)
P.O. Box 3709
Fairfax, VA 22038

Therapy Dogs International
6 Hilltop Road
Mendham, NJ 07945